3000 WORLD BUILDING PROMPTS

FROM
THE ART OF WORLD BUILDING
SERIES

RANDY ELLEFSON

Evermore Press
GAITHERSBURG, MARYLAND

Evermore Press, LLC
Gaithersburg, Maryland
www.evermorepress.org

3000 World Building Prompts / Randy Ellefson. – 1st Ed.
ISBN 978-1-946995-70-4 (paperback)

CONTENTS

ACKNOWLEDGEMENTS

Cover design by Randy Ellefson

Introduction

The Art of World Building series inspired all of the prompts in this book, so if you're struggling to answer a question, volumes 1-3 may help you find inspiration. These prompts are also organized by those volumes and chapters and presented in the same order.

About Me

By profession I'm a software developer, but I've been writing fantasy fiction since 1988 and building worlds just as long, mostly one planet called Llurien. Yes, I am crazy. But I love what I do. I didn't intend to work on it for so long, but when life has prevented me from writing, I've worked on Llurien. I've done everything in these chapters and authored two hundred thousand words of world building in my files. Llurien even has its own website now at http://www.llurien.com.

I've written several novels and more than a dozen short stories over the years, and began my publishing career with a novella that you can read for free (see below).

1

Also a musician with a degree in classical guitar, I've released instrumental rock albums, a classical guitar CD, and a disc of acoustic guitar instrumentals. You can learn more, hear songs, and see videos at my main website, http://www.randyellefson.com.

FREE BOOK

If you'd like to see a free sample of my own world building efforts in action, anyone who joins my fiction newsletter mailing list receives an eBook of *The Ever Fiend (Talon Stormbringer)*. Please note there's a separate newsletter for *The Art of World Building*, though both can be joined on the same signup form. Just check the box for each.

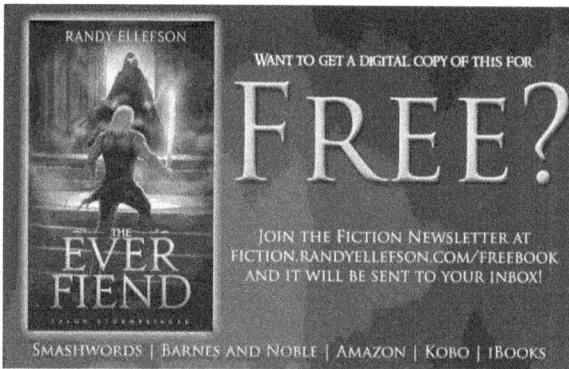

TEMPLATES AND NEWSLETTER

Effective world building requires having written down details about the created world. To help you organize and jumpstart your efforts, each volume in this series includes templates in the appendices. While these templates are not included in this book, you can download these templates for free by joining the newsletter for *The Art of World Building*. As each volume is published, whether you've bought the book or not, subscribers will automatically receive an email with links to download the templates as Microsoft Word files, which you can repeatedly use. Visit http://www.artofworldbuilding.com/newsletter/.

World Building University

World Building University (WBU) has online courses that provide step-by-step instruction on how to create all aspects of great fantasy and science fiction worlds. Each includes a series of video lessons, quizzes to test your retention of what you've learned, and assignments designed to make your creation a reality instead of a dream. Courses are intended for both authors, game designers, and hobbyists. A free course is available to get you started! See the website or mailing list for details:

http://www.worldbuilding.university/

The Podcast

The Art of World Building Podcast expands on the material within the series. The additional examples offer world builders more insight into ramifications of decisions. You can hear the podcast, read transcripts, and learn more about the episodes.

http://www.artofworldbuilding.com/podcasts.

YOUTUBE CHANNEL

The Art of World Building YouTube channel now has videos that also expand on the material within the series. Check out the growing playlists and subscribe. Videos include replays of webinars that feature a Q&A, lessons from the books, previews of WBU courses, and tips from the book, *185 Tips on World Building.*

    http://bit.ly/AOWBYouTube.

CHAPTER ONE

CREATING LIFE PROMPTS

Everything we need to know about how to create gods, species/races, plants, animals, monsters, heroes, villains, and even undead is included in *Creating Life (The Art of World Building, #1)*, which inspired the prompts in this section.

ANALOGUES

The following prompts come from Chapter 1.

1. Are you using an analogue?
2. What is your analogue primarily based on?
3. What three things can you change to make your analogue less recognizable?
4. Are you using a familiar name for your analogue, or inventing a new one for your creation?
5. What can you combine your analogue with to make it unique?

How Many Worlds

The following prompts come from Chapter 1 of *Creating Life*.

    6.   Do you intend to use this setting for more than one book series or a gaming campaign?

    7.   How many books will the series be?

    8.   How many worlds are in this story?

    9.   If multiple worlds, will you develop some more than others?

    10.   Is this an Earth-like planet or very different?

    11.   If different, in what ways is it so?

    12.   How do the differences affect the story?

    13.   Why do you want to make it different?

    14.   Does the setting have a significant impact on the story or could it almost be any fantasy or sci-fi setting?

The Gods

The following prompts come from Chapter 2 of *Creating Life*.

    15.   Do you want or need gods in the setting?

    16.   Are the gods real or imagined?

    17.   How many gods are there?

    18.   Are the gods part of a pantheon, like a family?

    19.   Are the gods equally powerful?

    20.   If not, how many tiers of power are there?

    21.   What is the difference in power level between tiers?

    22.   How many gods are in each tier?

23. Which ones are in each tier?

24. Do gods at different tiers have different rights and abilities?

25. Can gods go up or down a tier?

26. If so, what causes that to happen?

27. Has it ever happened before?

28. Are there are a set number of spots in a tier?

29. If so, why is that?

30. In order for someone to rise, must another fall?

31. How is the falling deity chosen?

32. Can they protest this?

33. What is the result of a dispute?

34. Who arbitrates the dispute?

35. Is a ruling binding or customarily followed?

36. Is one god considered the most powerful?

37. If so, who and why?

38. Has that always been the case?

39. Is one god considered the leader?

40. If so, who and why?

41. Has that always been the case?

42. How many pantheons of gods are there?

43. Are they equal in the number of gods or power levels and abilities?

44. Is one pantheon rising while another is falling?

45. What is causing their respective trajectories?

46. Is each god gender fluid or do they remain a specific gender?

47. Do the gods ever appear as animals?

48. If so, what is the rationale for their choice(s)?

49. Do they appear as objects that others can use?

50. Do they become more vulnerable in another form?

51. Do the gods have astrological signs? What are they?

MORTALITY

52. Are the gods able to reproduce?

53. Are some able to reproduce and others aren't?

54. Which ones and why?

55. Can the ability to reproduce be gained or lost? How?

56. Has it happened before? With whom?

57. How did this affect that deity and other gods?

58. What impact did this have on religions involving that god?

59. Can a god die?

60. If so, what happens to their powers?

61. Are they absorbed by other gods?

62. Are they just lost?

63. Does this impact the physical world directly, such as the god of storms losing control of weather?

64. Can all the gods die?

65. If so, does this precipitate the end of the world?

66. Or the end of an age?

67. Can they be reborn or resurrected?

68. How and by whom?

69. Can they be wounded?

70. Do they naturally regenerate and at what speed?

71. Can they be healed? How? By whom?

72. Where did the gods come from?

73. Were they themselves born of another being or the universe?

74. Did they make the universe?

RELATIONS

75. Do the gods interact with mortals?

76. If interacting with mortals is forbidden, what is the consequence to the deity?

77. Is any god suffering that consequence right now?

78. How are their followers affected by this?

79. What are some common swears that invoke a god's name?

80. Can the gods have offspring with other gods?

81. If so, are these other gods just as powerful or lesser?

82. Can the gods have offspring with mortals?

83. If so, what is the result?

84. Can the gods have offspring with animals?

85. If so, what is the result?

86. What is the creation myth?

87. Is there an end of times myth?

88. What is going to cause the end of times?

89. Are there famous stories of godly deeds or misdeeds?

90. If so, what lesson does each teach?

91. Are there stories about gods vs. gods or gods vs. a race?

92. How do the gods shed light on mortals and what concerns those mortals have?

93. Can a mortal become a god or a demi-god? How?

94. Are all or any of the gods associated with a season?

95. Are all or any of the gods associated with an element?

96. Do atheists exist or does everyone believe/know the god(s) are real?

97.   If atheists exist, what do any existing gods think of this?

98.   Does science peacefully exist beside faith?

99.   Are you basing any deities on an Earth analogue?

100. If using an analogue, what three changes can you make to have it appear different?

101. Where do the gods live?

102. Can mortals reach where the gods live?

103. Must mortals be invited to where the gods live?

104. What happens to a mortal who shows up where the gods live uninvited, unwanted, or unannounced?

105. Have the gods invented any interesting places and what is unique about them?

106. What role do gods play in the lives of non-gods?

A GOD

These prompts pertain to inventing a deity rather than general questions about gods.

107. What power(s) does the god have?

108. What is the god's gender?

109. Is the gender fluid or changeable?

110. Does the god have an animal form and if so, what is it?

111. What areas of concern does the deity have (love, war, etc.)?

112. What are the god's nicknames and titles?

113. What is the god's symbol?

114. Is the god the patron of anyone and who?

115. Is the god associated with a color?

116. Is there a specific day or month they are associated with or which is important to them or their followers and why?

117. Does the god have a specific item(s) associated with him or her? What properties does it have?

118. Is the god the only one who can use, or properly use, their items?

119. Has the god ever lost such an item and what was the result for the god and whoever found it?

120. Is the god considered a relative of anyone and in what way (sister, etc.)?

121. Does the god have any children?

122. Are the god's children gods, mortals, monsters, or a hybrid?

123. What is the god's relationship with offspring like?

124. Does this god get involved with mortals beyond answering prayers?

125. Does this god answer prayers?

126. What makes this god not answer a specific prayer?

127. Does this god require sacrifices?

128. If so, what kind and how often?

129. Is the god friendly or hostile?

130. Is this god temperamental?

131. How does the god behave?

132. Is the god good, evil, neither, or neutral?

133. Is the god or their followers feared?

134. Is the god mature or immature (spiteful, jealous, etc.)?

135. Where does this god live?

136. What is this god's home like?

137. Is that home separate from the other gods and why?

138. Are mortals able to visit this god and if so, how do they get there?

139. Is the home guarded and by what?

140. What is the god famous for?

141. Are their followers famous and for what?

142. Has the god created any lifeforms (species, animals, monsters)?

143. Has the god invented any objects?

144. Has the god created a place?

145. What caused the god to exist?

146. Does the god have parents?

147. Does the god have siblings?

148. Can this god be wounded?

149. Can this god die?

150. What kind of weapon or power can hurt or kill this god?

151. Has it recovered from a wound or death, or is there still a sign of this?

152. How old is the god?

153. Has the god participated in any wars between deities or mortals and in what capacity?

SPECIES

The following prompts come from Chapter 3 of *Creating Life*.

154. Will there be more than just humans in the setting?

155. How long have people been here?

156. Did they evolve here or come from somewhere else?

157. Does your answer apply equally to all species?

158. Are you using public domain races like elves and dwarves?

159. What is the reason for your choice?

160. What distinguishes your version of public domain races?

161. Are you going to use the usual word (like elf) for them?

162. Are you creating your own races/species?

163. Do you need to invent your own or want to, and why?

164. Do you want to mix yours with public domain ones?

165. If you use the word "race" to distinguish between elves and dwarves, for example, what word are you going to use to distinguish between black and white humans, for example?

A SPECIES/RACE

These prompts pertain to inventing a species/race. Remember to avoid a monoculture, meaning they're all the same; some of these prompts can be interpreted as making them all the same, but these are general questions to get us thinking, not a recommendation to create a monoculture. The words species and race are sometimes used interchangeably here, as the questions usually apply to inventing either.

166. Is this a species?

167. Or a race of a species?

168. How many members of this race/species will appear in the work?

169. If only one, do they represent the race very well or are they different from most?

170. How many populations exist in different geographical areas?

171. If you're going to use them to comment on humanity, what trait allows this and what aspect of humanity are you commenting upon?

172. Are you using an analogue to create them, and if so, what is it?

173. How does your invention differ from the analogue in three key ways?

174. Do you intend to use them as easy-to-kill inhabitants (think goblins)?

175. Do you intend them to be more fully fleshed out (like elves)?

176. What are they called?

177. Do they have nicknames?

178. What is their origin?

179. Did gods create them? If so, which one(s)?

180. Which gods do they often worship and why?

181. Have they discovered anything?

WORLD VIEW

182. Is their morality (good vs. evil) uniform or more nuanced like humanity?

183. If uniform, what actions cause them to be viewed as good or evil?

184. Are those actions indisputably bad/good or subtler and open to interpretation?

185. Are they viewed poorly because of cultural differences that lead to misunderstandings?

186. What are those differences and do they realize this is why others view them that way?

187. Is there a "good" race (wood elves) of the species and an "evil" one (dark elves)?

188. Do the good and evil versions look enough alike that they can impersonate each other?

189. How can someone truly tell them apart if so?

190. How skilled are they at impersonation?

191. Can they only fool someone in certain situations, in low light, or for a few minutes?

192. Is the race hostile to civilization?

193. Is the race forbidden anywhere?

194. How integrated with the world and other societies are they?

195. How frequently do they travel outside their homeland?

196. Are they found in great numbers elsewhere or just a few?

197. What kinds of places attract them in higher numbers?

198. Where they are welcomed, why is that?

199. If they are unwelcome, why is that?

200. What past incidents caused the response they receive?

201. Or are they distrusted because of reputation, misunderstanding, or another factor?

202. If they keep to themselves, why is that?

203. Do they welcome strangers or even friends to their homelands?

204. If welcoming, do they set aside areas to which other races are restricted?

205. What happened and with who?

206. How long ago?

207. Do some within their lands rebel against any isolation?

208. What effect has any isolation had on their world view and attitude toward strangers?

209. How are uninvited visitors to their settlements greeted?

210. If with hostility, are visitors killed on sight?

211. Are they jailed?

212. Enslaved?

213. Are they prone to fears and prejudice about other races?

214. What fears and prejudices do others express toward them?

215. How do they feel about the fears and prejudices others have toward them?

216. How tolerant are they of social diversity/issues?

RELATIONSHIPS AND FAMILY LIFE

217. Do they marry and at what age is considered young/old?

218. Is divorce possible?

219. Do people have more than one spouse? Are both genders able to or only one?

220. Do they have a written language?

221. If so, what form does it take (symbols, letters, etc.)?

222. What languages do they know?

223. How often do they give birth?

224. How long is pregnancy?

225. Are young born like people or in an egg?

226. Are twins, etc., common or uncommon?

227. How long do parents rear the children (to what age)?

228. Are both parents equally involved in child rearing?

229. When are children expected to leave the home?

230. When do children begin schooling and in what subjects?

231. Do they have higher education (college, technical school) or must they get it from another race?

232. Are children expected to take over a family business? What happens if they do not?

233. Is the first/last born treated better than others?

234. In combat, do they run or fight?

235. Do they only fight when they outnumber their opponents by a wide margin?

236. Do they engage in fights of honor?

237. Do they have any preferred or unique weapons?

238. Do they have calvary?

239. Are there any typical battle formations or plans?

240. What kinds of armor do they wear most often?

241. Do they have any unique defenses, whether from equipment or abilities?

242. Are they resistant to magic or supernatural or technological phenomenon (radiation)?

243. Is there anything they are afraid of?

244. If so, what is it and why?

245. Which other races are their consistent allies?

246. What other races are their consistent enemies?

247. With which races do they have a more variable relationship?

248. Are there any specific wars or battles in which they played a pivotal or memorable role?

HABITATS, SETTLEMENTS, AND HOME LIFE

249. Are they so welcoming of other species and people that they have furniture and even homes sized for other races?

250. What is the typical floor plan for homes and other buildings?

251. Are they distrustful or have they had poor experiences with others?

252. Are their settlements hidden?

253. Is anything done to erase an unwelcome visitor's memories of this place before setting them free somewhere?

254. Do they live in settlements others have built?

255. Have they built any settlements with other races?

256. If so, was it just because they lived in the same area?

257. Or was it a peace-making joint operation?

258. Was there another purpose behind it?

259. Does it still stand?

260. Are both still in power there?

261. If it was an experiment, has that failed or been a success?

262. Do they tend to be in positions of power, even in settlements or sovereign powers other species built?

263. If so, what traits cause this?

264. If not, are they often marginalized in another race's society?

265. Are there only specific races or nationalities that are unwelcome?

266. Do they have a long-standing feud with another race or nearby settlement?

267. What are their preferred habitats (forest, mountain)?

268. Are they afraid of open spaces from living somewhere enclosed? Or the opposite?

269. Do they dislike and avoid the sun or nighttime?

270. Is there a terrain that they prefer (mountains, forests)?

271. Why do they prefer that terrain? Does it give them an advantage and how?

272. Are there terrains they dislike?

273. If so, what causes this reaction and are they able to overcome it?

274. Is there a climate they prefer or avoid, or which makes them [un] comfortable?

275. What happens to their bodies or minds when exposed to it?

276. What are their sleeping habits?

277. How many meals do they need per day?

278. What kinds of food do they prefer or avoid?

279. Are they nomadic?

280. Do they live in tribes?

281. Do they farm?

282. Are they able to build homes and to what level of sophistication?

283. What sort of materials are homes and buildings constructed of (wood, stone, metal, glass)?

284. Are there are rooms with a specific function inside homes or other buildings?

285. Can they build towns and cities?

286. How many days of the week do they work?

287. How many hours a day do they work?

288. What is considered "normal" work schedules for the average person, to the point of society planning around it?

289. Do they take lunch breaks long enough to nap?

290. What do they do for fun?

Their Bodies

291. Has their preferred habitat impacted their bodies via adaptation?

292. Which adaptations have they made?

293. Can they see in the dark?

294. Do they have webbed toes and fingers?

295. Do they have a tail?

296. A forked tongue?

297. Which senses are heightened from their habitat?

298. Can they tolerate hot or cold temperatures better than humans?

299. What skin colors are predominant?

300. What in their habitat caused the skin color(s)?

301. Which other races judge them poorly or favorably for their skin color(s)?

302. How tall are they?

303. Has their average height changed in the last hundred years?

304. How fit are they?

305. Are skinny or overweight ones common or rare?

306. Has their average fitness changed in the last hundred years?

307. How long can they live?

308. How long do they typically live?

309. Is the lifespan better or worse now than before?

310. What hair colors are most common, or rare?

311. Is there a posture common to them?

312. Are they humanoid?

313. If so, are their faces round, oval, square, heart-shaped?

314. Are their brows prominent or shallow?

315. Are their eyebrows rounded, arched (and to what degree), or a mono brow?

316. Are their eyes round, slanted, deep set, up/down turned, wide/close set, hooded, protruding, or monoid?

317. Are their irises a vertical/horizontal slit, round, a cat's eye, or crescent?

318. What are typical eye colors?

319. Are their cheekbones sunken/indented, high/prominent, or low?

320. Are their noses straight, long and wide, hawkish, snub, thin and pointed, bulbous, upturned, aquiline, broad with large nostrils, or the basic large nose?

321. Are their mouths average, wide, small, full or thin lips (and are both the same?), rounded/pointed, or a Cupid's bow?

322. Are their teeth straight, crooked, missing, stained, pointed, serrated, poisonous, tiny, large, or multiple rows?

323. Are their chins protruding, cleft, thin and pointing, round, square, jutting, receding, or long?

324. Do they favor facial hair (and what type) or being clean shaven?

325. Are there common beard and mustache styles?

326. Do females also have beards?

327. Do females shave their legs (or anything else)?

328. Do males shave anything?

329. If not humanoid, what animal(s) is their body and head based on?

330. Are they capable of electro communication?

331. Do they have magnetoception?

332. Can they sense magical or supernatural energies?

333. How strong/weak is their hearing?

334. Can they hear things outside a human's hearing range?

335. Are they good/bad at distinguishing accents?

336. Do they hear well/poorly in noisy environments?

337. Are there any types of tastes they love or hate? Which ones?

338. Can they identify the source of a flavor?

339. Are they connoisseurs of food and drink?

340. Or will they consume just about anything?

341. What are they famous for loving?

342. What are they famous for hating?

343. Are their noses very sensitive?

344. If so, are they frequently used in tracking?

345. Are there any scents they find especially repugnant?

346. What smells do they love?

347. Do they sniff people as part of greeting them?

348. If so, are they discreet or blatant?

349. How do they react to those expressing discomfort with that?

350. Which of their five senses are the strongest/weakest and most/least relied upon?

351. What physical attributes (strength, agility, etc.) are strongest and weakest in them?

352. Are they athletic?

353. Do they have a higher or lower pain threshold than humans?

354. Do they have any non-humanoid features (like a tail)?

355. Do they have any innate supernatural abilities (like magic affinity)?

356. What distinguishes their clothing?

357. Are there items they typically wear (dress, tunics, kilts)?

358. Is clothing bright or drab?

359. Do they dress casually or formally?

360. Are clothes ill-fitting or tailored?

361. How stylized are clothes?

362. Are slogans and images on their attire?

363. Is clothing mismatched or a well-put together ensemble?

364. How much jewelry and what kind do they wear?

THEIR MINDS

365. What mental attributes (intelligence, charisma, etc.) are strongest and weakest in them?

366. How good is their morale?

367. Are they scholars?

368. Do they show a lot of skin or hardly any?

369. Are they okay with public nudity?

370. Do nude beaches exist?

371. If so, how frequently?

372. Do they act like the body is something to be ashamed of or proud of?

373. What makes people feel shamed? Too much/little weight or something else?

374. What forms of government are they capable of?

375. What forms of government are most common?

376. Do they have any sixth sense?

377. Are they capable of telepathy?

378. Clairvoyance?

379. Telekinesis?

380. Mediumship?

381. Psychometry?

382. Remote viewing?

383. For each, how strong are they in the ability?

384. How common is the ability?

385. Are the abilities innate or can they be learned?

386. Is there an age when the ability first manifests?

387. Is there an age when they are expected to have mastered it?

388. Do their abilities cause a fearful reaction among their own kind?

389. Among others?
390. Have they always had these abilities or are they recent?
391. If recently, what caused them?
392. What effect do these have on their culture?

Magic and Technology

393. Are they technologically advanced or inferior to others in the setting?
394. Can they invent technology and at what level of sophistication?
395. Can they train others/themselves in technology or must they get training from someone else?
396. Can they operate technology others have designed?
397. What role does technology play in their society and lives?
398. Are they capable of magic if it exists in the setting?
399. Are they afraid of magic?
400. How skilled with magic can they be?
401. Are they able to invent spells?
402. What role does magic play in their society and lives?
403. Are they able to train others/themselves or must they get training from someone else?
404. If there are different types of magic, which ones can/can't they do and why?
405. Is there a limit on how powerful they can become in magic?
406. Have they invented anything?

WORLD FIGURES

The following prompts come from Chapter 4 of *Creating Life*.

407. What kind of figure are you creating (hero, villain, martyr, etc.)?

408. What is their name and does it mean anything?

409. What nicknames do they have? How did they earn the name(s)?

410. What species or race are they?

411. Are you going to use this person as a main or minor character?

412. Or are you only mentioning them and they do not appear in the story?

413. What kind of person admires this figure?

414. What kind of person hates this figure?

415. What are they famous/infamous for?

416. What significant deeds have they done?

417. What event turned them into a world figure?

418. Who or what was involved in this?

419. Are they a reluctant figure or someone who sought it out?

420. What stories about them are true?

421. What stories about them are false and in what way?

422. What is unknown about them?

423. What places have heard of them?

424. Do they regret their fame?

425. If their fame has faded, how do they feel about that?

Status

426. Are they alive or dead?

427. If dead, how long has that been true?

428. What/who killed them?

429. How did they die?

430. Is their death indisputable, or is there a chance they're still alive somewhere?

431. How old are/were they?

432. Are they free or imprisoned? Hiding? Living peacefully?

433. What weapons, armor, or items did they have that are worth people remembering and/or coveting?

434. What is special about those items?

435. Are any magical?

436. Is an item broken, the pieces scattered and awaiting reconstruction?

437. If so, where are the pieces?

438. Who is searching for this and what do they hope will happen from finding it?

439. Was there an animal associated with them, like a steed?

440. Did/do they have a ship?

441. How is it noteworthy? Just because it is theirs?

442. Or does it have unusual speed or weaponry?

443. Does it have hidden compartments or other unexpected features?

444. Where is it now?

Relationships

445. Are their parents still alive?

446. If so, what is their relationship?

447. Do they have a romantic partner?

448. If so, who is/was it?

449. Are/were they married/divorced?

450. Is that person alive or dead?

451. Do they have children?

452. Do they know about their children?

453. Are the children alive or dead?

454. How old are the children, and what genders?

455. Do the children know this person is their father/mother or have they heard of him/her?

456. What does each person in the family think of this figure?

457. And what does he think of them?

458. Have any of the people close to them been targeted by their enemies?

459. Has this targeting changed the world figure's behavior?

460. Have any of them been kidnapped?

461. Killed?

462. Held for ransom?

463. What effect did this have on the world figure?

464. Have any of these people come after the world figure to change their behavior?

465. Did it work?

466. Did it strengthen or end the relationship?

467. What does each race/species in the setting think of this figure, who can be a hero to some and a villain to others?

ABILITIES

468. What is/was their profession?

469. What skills do they have?

470. Where did they learn their skills?

471. Are those who taught them still around?

472. If so, what do they think of what this world figure does with his/her skills?

473. Would the figure be welcomed back by those trainers?

474. Do they have street smarts?

475. Book smarts?

476. How well-traveled are they?

477. What situations can they blend into?

478. In what situations do they immediately stand out?

APPEARANCE

479. Do they have any identifiable scars?

480. What is their hair color and length?

481. What is their eye color?

482. What is their overall build?

483. What impression do they create on sight?

484. What impression do they create when they speak?

485. What sort of attire do they wear?

486. What colors do they wear?

MONSTERS

The following prompts come from Chapter 5 of *Creating Life*.

487. Does the monster have a name?

488. Does it have a nickname?

489. Are you using your monster to teach a moral lesson and if so, what is it?

490. Is the monster real or just a story?

491. What kinds of people don't believe it exists?

492. Is the monster known or unknown?

493. If it's famous, for what?

494. What does it look like?

495. Is the monster hideous or attractive?

496. Is it humanoid?

497. Was the monster once a species? Which one?

498. Is there any of its "humanity" left? How much and what parts?

499. How much of its intelligence or knowledge does it maintain?

500. How does it feel about what it is now?

501. What exaggerations do people make about it and what is actually true?

502. What sorts of stories do people tell about it?

503. How does it feel about its appearance and how people react to it?

504. How do people react to the sight of it or its presence?

IT'S LIFE

505. Is there only one of them?

506. Can it reproduce and how?

507. How many offspring are produced at once?

508. Are offspring born in an egg?

509. Are offspring immediately dangerous and how?

510. Do offspring get more dangerous later and in what stages?

511. Does it need a mate to reproduce?

512. Is there a master monster who controls others?

513. If the master is killed, do the subordinates die?

514. Is the master also a monster or a race?

515. How can it be killed?

516. How hard or easy is it to be killed?

517. When dismembered, do the parts continue to move or become additional monsters?

518. Is a special weapon needed to hurt or kill it?

519. Was this monster the result of an accident?

520. If so, who or what caused the accident?

521. Did magic cause the monster?

522. Did someone create this monster on purpose? Why?

523. Is the monster a product of nature or a phenomenon?

524. What caused its evolution into its current form?

525. Where is the source of this evolution?

526. Is that source capable of creating more?

527. Would each one be the same?

528. Does anyone know the answer to that?

529. How long ago was the monster created?

530. Do people know where the monster came from? Is the backstory known?

531. Is there anyone trying to understand this monster?

532. Who are they and why do they care?

533. What is the monster's lifespan?

534. Is there a god protecting this monster?

535. What does the monster consume to survive?

536. Does it consume anything for pleasure?

537. Are species/races on the menu?

MOTIVES AND BEHAVIOR

538. Does the monster just want to survive?

539. Does the monster want to hoard treasure? And why?

540. Does the monster just want to be safe and left alone?

541. Does the monster want revenge and for what?

542. Is there a known expert in its history or behavior?

543. Does the monster have a god?

544. Does the monster work with a god or at their behest?

545. How smart is the monster?

546. Does the monster understand what actions of it will cause people to seek it out and attempt to destroy it?

547. Does it want to lure people to it and why? To consume them?

548. Does the monster consume people?

549. Does the monster do anything else to people?

550. Does the monster have unusual strength?

551. Can the monster withstand unusual amounts of pain or injury?

552. Can the monster regenerate body parts or otherwise recover from wounds?

553. Is the monster faster or slower than usual?

554. Is the monster mobile or rooted to a spot?

555. Does the monster have better/worse endurance?

556. Can it travel faster or farther than expected?

557. Is it faster or slower in combat?

558. Does its body inhibit the way it moves and attacks?

559. Can it chase down prey?

560. How much control does it have with weapons?

561. Can it fire a gun or crossbow?

562. Is the monster afraid of anything? Enough that it will flee?

563. What unique skills does the monster have?

564. What does the monster think of those living nearby?

565. What impact does the monster have on society?

566. Do people avoid traveling near where it is rumored to be, or with reinforcements?

567. Does the monster understand any languages?

568. Does the monster speak any languages?

569. Can the monster write a language or have its own?

570. Does the monster mark its territory and how?

571. Does it have any habits, like stacking bones?

572. Does it do anything at predictable intervals?

573. How does it get along with each species/race?

574. How does the monster track victims?

575. Does the monster attract prey?

576. How does the monster prefer to kill?

577. What does the monster do with victims?

578. What can the monster do that is noteworthy and defining?

579. Is it adept at hiding?

580. Does the monster have any supernatural abilities?

581. Can it perform magic and to what level?

582. What kind of magic can it do?

583. Is it afraid of magic?

584. Does it have a supernatural place nearby?

585. Can the monster use technology and to what degree?

586. Does the monster have a lair?

587. What makes a suitable lair?

588. Can it build or change a place into a suitable lair?

589. What type of terrain does it prefer or is commonly found in?

590. What type of climate does it exist in?

591. Are there bodies of victims in its lair? Where they fell or were they stacked?

592. Does the monster stay in its lair? What percentage of time?

593. How far from its lair does it travel?

594. Does it have more than one lair and why? What distinguishes each?

595. Is it looking for a home right now?

596. Does it have a particular place it prefers, such as a cave or an abandoned settlement?

597. Is the monster nocturnal?

598. How does the monster fight?

599. Does the monster use weapons, or only its limbs, teeth, etc.?

600. Does the monster rely on brute force?

601. Is the monster cunning?

602. Does it have any special attacks?

PLANTS

The following prompts come from Chapter 6 of *Creating Life*.

603. What is the plant's name?

604. Is this plant based on an Earth analogue?

605. If this plant is seedless, is it algae, a liverwort, a moss, or a fern?

606. If the plant has seeds, is it a cycad, conifer, or flowering plant?

607. If a flowering plant, is it a flower, shrub, vine, or a tree like the oak, maple, elm, aspen, or birch?

608. Can this plant be used to create medicines?

609. What kind of medicine and which part of the plant?

610. Is this plant used for decoration?

611. Do people eat this plant and if so, how is it prepared?

612. What does this plant taste like?

613. Is any part of this plant poisonous?

614. Is this a delicacy?

615. Is eating it forbidden to anyone?

616. What other products result from this plant?

617. Are there any stories about this plant and its uses?

618. Is it difficult to harvest?

619. Does the plant grow in only unusual or hard to reach places?

620. How common is this plant?

621. How valuable is this plant?

622. What climate does this plant grow in?

623. In what season is it planted and harvested?

624. What does the plant smell like?

625. If a flower, how many petals does it have?

626. What color(s) are any petals?

627. Are any birds, bees, or other animals especially attracted to this?

628. If a tree, how tall does it grow?

629. What color are its leaves?

630. Does it grow at higher altitudes?

631. How much shade or full sun does it require?

632. What impression does the plant create?

633. As its creator, what uses do you have for it?

634. How often will you be able to use or mention it?

635. How often will people of the world be able to use it?

ANIMALS

The following prompts come from Chapter 6 of *Creating Life.*

636. What is the animal's name?

637. Is this animal based on an Earth analogue?

638. When is the animal active?

639. Is this animal an invertebrate (worms, sea urchins, jellyfish, snails, arachnids, crustaceans, corals, or insects)?

640. Is this animal a vertebrate (amphibian, bird, fish, mammal, or reptile)?

641. If a bird, does it migrate?

642. If so, to and from where?

643. Is it a flightless bird?

644. What is its plumage?

645. Can it be used to carry messages?

646. Can the bird be used to hunt?

647. If amphibious, is it [like] a frog, toad, or salamander?

648. Can it breathe through its skin?

649. How many appendages does it have and what are they?

650. What does it look like?

651. Does it have hair? Where on its body? What color(s)?

652. Can this animal be used to create medicines? What kind and which part of the animal?

653. Is this animal used for decoration?

654. Do people eat this animal and if so, which parts and how is it prepared?

655. What does this animal taste like?

656. Is any part of this animal poisonous?

657. Is it venomous?

658. What is the antidote?

659. Is this a delicacy?

660. Is eating it forbidden to anyone?

661. Can this animal be used for entertainment (such as horse racing)?

662. Does this animal make a good guard?

663. Is this animal kept as a pet?

664. Is this animal ridden?

665. Can this animal be used to pull wagons, etc.?

666. What products result from this animal?

667. Can part of this animal be used as a weapon?

668. Are there any stories about this animal and its uses?

669. How common is it?

670. How valuable is it?

671. What climates does this animal prefer?

672. What terrains does it prefer?

673. What are some specific places it is found?

674. What does the animal smell like?

675. Is it a solitary or pack animal (and how large is a pack)?

676. Can it be domesticated?

677. Is it tamable?

678. Is it trainable and to what degree?

679. Is it a carnivore, omnivore, or herbivore?

680. Does it eat people? On purpose or by accident?

681. Under what circumstances will it attack someone?

682. How does it attack?

683. How likely is a fatal attack?

684. Does it lay eggs or do live birth?

685. How many offspring are born at once?

686. How frequently does it give birth?

687. How long is pregnancy?

688. How long does the mother raise the young?

689. What does this animal prey on?

690. What animals prey on this animal?

691. Do people prey on this animal?

692. Do people make trophies from it?

693. Is this animal's name used as a nickname for people?

694. What is valuable about this animal's body parts, and which ones?

695. Do people make clothing from it (like furs)?

696. Do people make tools from it?

697. Is it feared?

698. As its creator, what uses do you have for it?

699. How often will you be able to use or mention it?

700. How often will people of the world be able to use it?

UNDEAD

The following prompts come from Chapter 7 of *Creating Life*.

701. Is this undead similar to a public domain one and in what ways?

702. How does this undead different from a public domain idea?

703. What is the proper name for this undead?

704. What are its nicknames?

705. It is a spiritual or corporeal undead?

706. If corporeal, does it have a soul?

707. What state of decay is the body?

708. How are each of its senses affected?

709. Can it see well in the dark?

710. Does it have heat vision?

711. How mobile is it?

712. Is it capable of appearing as if it's alive instead of undead (like vampires)?

713. What does it look like?

714. If a spirit, does it retain an image of itself as healthy and alive, appearing that way?

715. Or does its appearance reveal that it is dead, such as showing wounds or decay?

716. Is it typically aware that it is dead or undead?

717. It is humanoid, animal, plant, or other?

718. Did it originate from an accident?

719. Did a phenomenon (like radiation) cause it?

720. Did magic or technology/science lead to its existence?

721. Did someone create it on purpose and why? Who?

722. When did it first come to exist?

723. Is it capable of turning others into something just like it via a bite or touch?

724. What can prevent someone from becoming one of them? Is that known?

725. Are there any talismans or symbols that are known (or believed) to frighten or wound it?

726. Are people wrong about that and to what degree?

727. How long until someone/something else becomes one once exposed to the triggering incident?

728. Must someone die before becoming this type of undead?

729. How long does something have to be dead before becoming this?

730. How many of them exist in general or in a particular area?

731. What sort of weapon or item is needed to wound or kill it?

732. Is it afraid of anything? Why?

733. Can it be rendered immobile, possibly so that people think it's dead when it isn't?

734. Can it feign death (on purpose)?

735. Can it be killed? How?

736. What happens to one that is destroyed?

737. Does it prefer graveyards?

738. Does it haunt places?

739. Does it haunt people?

740. What are some specific places it is known to be found?

741. Is it solitary or found in packs (of what quantity)?

742. If it has a home, what kind?

743. How far from or near to civilization can it typically be found?

744. What brings it out of hiding?

745. What makes it go back into hiding?

746. Can it be summoned? How?

747. When summoned, how difficult/easy is it for the summoner to control?

748. Does it have feelings about having been summoned and what are they?

749. How likely is it for the summoner to lose control of it?

750. How likely is it for the undead to attack and/or kill the summoner?

751. How intact is its mind?

752. Is it delusional or crazy?

753. Is it sinister?

754. Can they communicate with each other, and to what degree of sophistication?

755. Can it speak?

756. Or does it only make unintelligible sounds?

757. Does it understand languages and which ones?

758. Can it read?

759. What does it want? Revenge?

760. To inflict pain or horror?

761. To finish a task that remained unfinished at death?

762. What happens when this goal is achieved?

763. What does it need to continue existing (food), and how often?

764. What happens if it is deprived of what it needs?

765. What can it do?

766. What can it not do?

767. How fast is it?

768. How strong is it?

769. How agile is it?

770. Can it perform magic?

771. Can it manipulate technology?

772. How does it fight?

773. Does it have any famous attacks or defenses?

774. Do biological scanners and other devices work on it?

775. If spiritual, can this move through solid objects?

776. Is there anything it cannot pass through?

777. Who does it prey upon?

778. What does it do to victims? Just kill them? Turn them into one?

779. What do people know about this undead?

780. Can its behavior be predicted?

781. As its creator, how are you going to use it?

782. How rare is it?

CHAPTER TWO

CREATING PLACES PROMPTS

The life we create needs to originate from somewhere on a planet. *Creating Places (The Art of World Building, #2)* inspired the prompts in this section.

PLANETS

The following prompts come from Chapter 2.

783. What is the name of the galaxy?

784. What is the solar system's name?

785. Are there any comets and how often do they appear?

786. Is there an asteroid field?

787. If so, in between which planets is it found?

788. How hard is it to pilot through it?

789. Are there any destroyed planets in this system?

790. If so, is the planet in pieces?

791. Or is just devoid of livable conditions now?

792. What kind of sun (yellow, red dwarf) is at the system's center?

793. Is it a binary star system?

794. How many planets are in the solar system?

795. Which planet are you creating (nearest, farthest, fourth)?

796. Does the planet have a ring system (like Saturn)?

797. Is the atmosphere breathable?

798. Is this a rocky, icy, or gaseous planet?

799. How many seasons are there and how often do they occur?

800. Is the planet in a retrograde orbit of the sun?

801. Does the planet rotate clockwise or counter-clockwise?

802. Are there other planets in the solar system?

803. What do they look like to the naked eye from this planet, if they can be seen?

804. How many planets are in the sun's habitable zone?

805. Can other planets be seen with the naked eye?

806. Can other planets be visited via magic or techno-logical means?

807. Are any constellations important in your setting?

808. Which constellations are visible in each hemi-sphere?

809. Are there are dark constellations?

810. Are there constellations associated with months, like astrological signs?

811. Is this planet bigger or smaller than Earth and by how much?

812. Has global warming occurred and to what degree?

MOONS

813. How many moons are there?

814. Are any of the moons tidally locked?

815. Is the planet and one moon tidally locked to each other?

816. Are any moons in a retrograde orbit?

817. Are any moons barren?

818. Are any moons icy?

819. Are the tides the moon(s) cause bigger, smaller, or the same as on Earth?

820. How many moons are causing the tides? If more than one, how often do the biggest tides occur?

821. Are there any conjunctions of moons, planets and the sun(s) and how often do these occur?

822. Are any moons habitable? Which ones?

HABITABLE MOONS

823. Is the world you're creating right now a moon?

824. If so, what effect(s) does the planet have on it?

825. How often does the planet cast its shadow over the moon in a penumbral eclipse?

826. In a total lunar eclipse?

827. In a partial lunar eclipse?

828. How dark does it get during each of these eclipse types?

829. For how long does this occur?

830. Are there any natural events that take place then, such as creatures who only come out at that time?

831. How does this impact sentient life on the moon?

832. Are there any rituals or protections people plan for and make?

CONTINENTS

The following prompts come from Chapter 3 of *Creating Places*.

833. How many continents are you creating?

834. How many will figure prominently in your work right now?

835. Which one are you creating as you read these prompts? What is its name?

836. Which continents are near this one, in what direction, and how far?

837. How difficult is each nearby continent to reach from this one?

838. How can people reach other continents?

839. What is this continent famous for?

840. Is this continent feared?

841. Are people from this continent feared?

842. Is the wildlife considered more dangerous or safer here?

843. Are plants here considered more exotic?

844. Which hemisphere is this continent on, or does it straddle the equator?

845. What percentage is above and below the equator?

846. Are there any large islands offshore?

847. Is there a chain of volcanic islands offshore?

848. Is there just one volcanic island?

849. Is there a lone volcano anywhere on the continent?

850. Where are the explosive mountain ranges?

851. Where are the taller/shorter ranges?

852. Are there any straits here?

853. Are there any river deltas?

854. Are there any large bays?

855. Is there a sea here?

856. Is this continent connected to another by a narrow area of land? Was it once? How long ago?

857. Where is the longest river?

858. Where is the most widely used river(s) for travel and commerce?

859. Where are the oldest and youngest rivers?

860. Where is the largest lake?

861. What regions exist, as defined by terrain and/or climates?

862. What is the climate in each region?

863. For civilizations, are the oldest or youngest found here?

864. Where are the sovereign powers located?

865. What areas do not have a sovereign power controlling them?

866. How heavily fished are the oceans and rivers?

867. Is toxic waste being dumped and where? What effect has it had?

868. Have dams been created?

869. What rivers have been diverted?

870. Are earthquakes common on this continent and in what areas?

871. When was the last major earthquake?

872. Are tornadoes common on this continent and in what areas?

873. Do monsoon rains happen here?

874. If so, where?

875. Which months of the year does it occur?

876. Is there a hurricane season here and when is it?

877. What parts of the continent are impacted?

878. Are tsunamis common? On which coastlines?

879. When was the last major tsunami?

880. Are hailstones common and where, if so?

881. Does anywhere experience lake effect snows or unusual blizzards? Where?

882. What areas experience drought?

883. How long has the last drought been occurring?

884. Is there an area prone to wildfires? Where are they?

885. What areas are prone to flooding?

886. Are any areas that are near to deserts prone to dust or sandstorms?

887. If so, during which months?

888. Do people flee from these phenomena?

889. Do they build shelters or ride it out?

890. Has there been a meteor strike in recent memory?

891. Is there a visible crater anywhere and where?

892. When was the most massive loss of life from one of these disasters?

Land Features

The following prompts come from Chapter 4 of *Creating Places*.

893. How cultivated or terraformed is the land?

894. Have deserts been turned into settlements?

895. Have forests been burned down?

896. Have mountains been leveled?

897. Are there significant canyons anywhere and what makes them so? Size? Formation? Beauty? Adventure? Beasts?

898. For grasslands, are there nomadic tribes living here?

899. Are they thought to be savages?

FOR ALL LAND FEATURES

These prompts should be viewed when creating mountains, forests, or other landscapes.

900. What is its name?
901. What is its nickname(s)?
902. Will you use this as a setting that characters interact with or only as framing?
903. What continent is it on?
904. Are there any stories about the landscape?
905. Does this act as the border between lands or sovereign powers?
906. Does more than one sovereign power border this or lay claim to all or part of it? Where?
907. Are any unique plants or animals found within?
908. Are any common plants or animals found within?
909. Is there a monster there?
910. Is anything particularly abundant or rare/valuable here?
911. How safe or dangerous is it here? Does this vary by region?
912. Do people disappear inside this land feature and never return?
913. Do you know what happens to them?
914. Does anyone on the world know?
915. Are there any humanoid species/races living here?
916. Is there a famous fortress or settlement here? Where is it?
917. Are there watch towers here? What features do they typically include?
918. Are there any roads passing through it?
919. What quality are the roads and who built them?

920. Did anything interesting make the trails found here?

921. Is there anything particularly dangerous or friendly dwelling here?

922. Are there bandits?

923. Are there inns or taverns?

924. Are people afraid of traveling through here? Why?

925. Have any ruins within been discovered? What is their backstory?

926. Are there any settlements within?

MOUNTAINS

927. Is this a lone mountain or a range?

928. If a range, what direction is it (north/south, etc.)?

929. Is it volcanic? How many peaks of it are?

930. How tall are the mountains?

931. What are the names of the tallest or more interesting peaks?

932. Are there any flying creatures or machines that struggle to get over it?

933. Are mining operations taking place?

934. If so, what is found here in unusual quantities?

935. What is not known to be found here but is?

936. Are there any mountain passes and where are they?

937. How difficult is it to travel through the passes?

938. How hard is it to cross the mountains without using a pass?

939. Do people live underground here?

940. Is there a kind of building stone that is found here and commonly/rarely used?

941. For every volcano, is it active, dormant, or extinct?

942. When was the last eruption?

943. How devastating was it and was life altered for any species, settlement(s), or sovereign powers? Or even the world?

944. Did the volcano unleash anything unusual?

FORESTS

945. Is this a forest, savannah, woodland, or jungle?

946. Is this forest used for horseback riding?

947. Do people hunt here?

948. How close to a settlement is it?

949. When was the last major fire and in what area of the forest?

950. Is there a Forest Service that manages the health of the forest?

951. If this is a jungle, how impenetrable is it?

WETLANDS

952. Where is this wetland located?

953. Is this a mire, bog, swamp, or marsh?

954. How close to a settlement is it?

955. If a mire, how much of the top is covered by peat?

Deserts

956. Is this a hot, cold, or mild desert?
957. Is this desert rocky or sandy?
958. At what elevation is it found?
959. How close to a settlement is it?
960. Do settlements have underground areas?
961. Is there any grass here, making this a steppe?
962. How much rainfall occurs every year?

Sovereign Powers

The following prompts come from Chapter 5 of *Creating Places*.

963. What is the name of this sovereign power?
964. Are there any nicknames for it?
965. Will you set scenes here or only mention this place?
966. Will characters be from here?
967. Is there a state religion?
968. Has this power built/destroyed anything and what/why?
969. And what did people think of that?
970. What is the power famous/infamous for?
971. Is this power feared and by whom?
972. Is this power admired and for what?
973. Is this power influential and in what way(s)?
974. Who is a famous/infamous resident?
975. Which products is the power known for producing?
976. What is the power's symbol?
977. What are the power's official colors?

978. Does the power have a slogan?

979. How old is it?

980. Which parts of it existed first?

981. What are the primary world views of this power?

982. Does the world view of those in power conflict with that of the population, or major portions of it?

983. Does the world view today differ from the world view espoused by the power's creators?

984. If so, how are these differences affecting daily life and tensions?

POPULATION

985. Which species created this power?

986. What percentage of each species lives here?

987. Are any species outlawed or discriminated against and why?

988. Are there areas where some species are found in but not others?

989. Which race's culture dominates this power?

990. Is this a highly populated power?

991. What ethnic groups live in each region?

992. Is there an official language and what is it?

993. What languages are spoken here?

994. Are any languages restricted/forbidden and why?

995. Have the dominant languages changed so that older ones are still inscribed in public places or possibly defaced as a result?

996. What sort of freedoms exist here?

997. What restrictions of freedoms exist here?

998. In recent years, is the population shifting from rural to urban or vice versa?

999.   How much immigration from other powers is occurring?

1000.   Which way is the immigration happening? Are more people coming than going? What is the reason?

1001.   To/from which other powers is this happening and in what percentages?

1002.   How do people feel about foreigners?

1003.   Which areas have the most foreigners?

1004.   Why do they congregate there, or is the government controlling that? Why?

1005.   Why do foreigners come here?

1006.   Is there a dream or vision of what life will be like?

1007.   Is that met with reality or not?

1008.   Who is responsible for creating the dream and any disparity between it and reality?

1009.   Are all foreigners treated equally or are some considered better than others?

1010.   Are some reduced to menial labor? Which ones?

1011.   Is the discrimination based on race, class, or another factor?

1012.   Are there any restrictions on carrying or using weapons?

1013.   What do people do for fun?

1014.   What games are common or rare?

1015.   How common is crime in the power?

1016.   How tall do people tend to be here?

1017.   How fit are they?

1018.   What hair colors are common and what stands out?

1019.   What about eye colors?

Government

1020.   If this is an authoritative state, is it an autocracy, totalitarian, dictatorship, or authoritarian government?

1021.   If the latter, is the state only concerned with controlling political aspects, or do they also control other elements of society? Which ones and to what degree?

1022.   Do people routinely disappear?

1023.   If this is a dictatorship, who is the dictator and how did they come to power?

1024.   How do they maintain power?

1025.   Is the dictator only a figurehead controlled by an inner circle?

1026.   If so, who comprises the inner circle?

1027.   What do they want?

1028.   How long has the dictator been in power?

1029.   Is this a stable or unstable dictatorship?

1030.   Is this part of an empire, federation, confederation, or unitary state?

1031.   If so, what can they self-govern? What can't they?

1032.   Can this power voluntarily leave?

1033.   Are they in good standing?

1034.   What countries are currently in it?

1035.   What sovereign powers left and how long ago?

1036.   What happened when they left and why did they?

1037.   If this is an empire, how long has it existed? When did it first conquer another power, and which one was it?

1038.   Which powers does it control now?

1039.   Have any powers left the empire and what happened when they did?

1040.   Is there an empire that has fallen?

1041.   If so, what aspects of modern life are still influenced by it?

1042.   Is the empire still expanding or is it in decline?

1043.   If this is a monarchy, is it an absolute or constitutional one?

1044.   If constitutional, who is the Prime Minister?

1045.   Are there other ministers (Minister of Magic) and what are their titles and roles?

1046.   Does the divine right of kings exist here?

1047.   What is the line of succession and is it currently under dispute?

1048.   Is this an oligarchy, and what kind (theocracy, aristocracy, military junta, etc.)?

1049.   If this is a democracy, what laws are supposed to apply to everyone but don't?

1050.   Is the balance of power in the democracy under threat?

1051.   Is this democracy one that others aspire to be like?

1052.   Is this a direct democracy or indirect?

1053.   Is this a parliamentary or presidential democracy?

1054.   What are the major political parties?

1055.   What are their agendas?

1056.   Are the parties currently functional or dysfunctional?

1057.   Is the government paralyzed by political fighting?

1058.   Is there a new political force?

1059.   If so, what is its agenda?

1060.   How successful or disruptive is it?

1061.   What ideas are considered conservative or liberal?

1062.   Are people satisfied with the government or disgusted?

1063.   What societal ills persist?

1064.   What special interest groups hold influence and to what end, and is this known?

1065. How is time measured here? What event is Year 1 to them?

1066. What events led to its form of government?

1067. How long has this been the form of government?

1068. What is the most previous form of government?

1069. Is the head of state a different person than the head of government?

1070. Who is currently head of state?

1071. Who is currently the head of government?

1072. Can the head of government sign laws into existence by themselves?

1073. Can they be booted from office? By congress or a popular vote?

1074. Are they protected from prosecution?

1075. Can they be executed? Has one? Who and for what?

1076. Can they raise and lower taxes?

1077. Do they need permission or cooperation from others in government to get things done?

1078. Can they get away with conflicts of interest?

1079. Can they declare war?

1080. Can they suppress or oppress the media, communications, and the people?

1081. Are there exceptions to any of this?

1082. Who takes over if the head of government is incapacitated?

1083. Is the head of state ceremonial only or do they keep some powers? Which ones?

1084. How much conflict exists between the head of state and the head of government?

1085. Do residents respect or like the head of state?

1086. Do residents respect or like the head of the government?

1087. Which sovereign powers recognize this one is sovereign?

1088.   Which sovereign power does not recognize that this one is sovereign?

1089.   Are there groups within this power that dispute its sovereignty?

1090.   Is there a territory within it where sovereignty is disputed?

1091.   What aspects of life does the government control?

1092.   What services (such as school, drinking water) does the government provide?

MAGIC AND TECHNOLOGY

1093.   Is magic championed, outlawed, or something in between?

1094.   How technologically advanced is this power?

1095.   Are any technologies outlawed or championed here?

1096.   Has this power been given credit for a magical or technological invention or discovery and what is it?

1097.   Is magic or technological training available?

1098.   If so, in what?

1099.   How extensive is it?

1100.   Do people come here for it or go elsewhere for it?

1101.   Is this power considered formidable because of either?

1102.   Where is the center of magical or technological power?

MILITARY MIGHT

1103.   Is this a seafaring power?

1104.   Is this a spacefaring power?

1105.   Is this a military power?

1106.   How well trained is the military?

1107.   How well organized is the military?

1108.   Are there standing forces or must an army be cobbled together when needed?

1109.   Which races are allowed/forbidden in the military?

1110.   Which armed forces types are here (army, navy, knights, etc.)?

1111.   What level of fortifications is the power capable of?

1112.   For either, is it dominant or dominated, and with who?

1113.   Has it conquered other territories or powers, or lost them, and from/to whom?

1114.   Does it covet any location, and why?

1115.   Has a famous battle involved this power and in what way?

1116.   Are the weapons and defenses of this power superior, inferior, or the same as allies and enemies?

1117.   What sort of siege engines are available?

1118.   What weapons of mass destruction are available?

1119.   Is there such a thing as a war crime or is it anything goes?

1120.   How much spying takes place within this country?

1121.   Are the targets of spying domestic and foreign?

1122.   Is the spying in person or magical/technological?

1123.   How are caught spies treated?

Location

1124.   Which continent(s) is the power on?

1125.   If multiple, where did it start, and to where did it expand?

1126.   Where on the continent(s) is it?

1127.   Is it landlocked?

1128.   Does it control the entire continent/planet?

1129.   Are there nameable regions?

1130.   What are the climates in each region?

1131.   What land features/terrain are with in it?

1132.   Are there any land features or terrain that don't exist within its territory?

1133.   What land features border it and where?

1134.   Does it dispute control over a land feature?

1135.   Is a land feature important to it and why?

1136.   What is the capital and where is it?

1137.   What are the major settlements and their location?

1138.   What unique places exist within the power?

1139.   What are the most common points of entry for visitors?

1140.   How hard is it to immigrate here? Why?

1141.   Is there a sacred site here, such as a significant battle location?

1142.   What resources lie within the territory of this power?

1143.   Which of them are rare?

1144.   Are any of them in contested lands and if so, who is contesting it?

1145.   What is the strength of this contest?

1146.   How is that contested territory being handled?

1147.   Is this important enough that war looms or has broken out before?

1148.   How recently, if ever, has this territory changed hands and with whom?

RELATIONSHIPS

1149.   Are there any organizations that have a foothold here, and why?

1150.   Have any organizations been eradicated?

1151.   Are any organizations trying to gain a foothold and why?

1152.   With what sovereign powers does this one have good/poor relations with and why?

1153.   What powers border this one and where are they located?

1154.   Are there ambassadors for other powers?

1155.   If so, are there laws dictating what rights ambassadors have?

1156.   What happens when those laws are violated?

1157.   Do ambassadors from other powers have designated homes or territory in this one?

1158.   What are the existing treaties between this and other powers?

BUSINESS AND WORK

1159.   Are imports and exports tightly controlled?

1160.   Do businesses need a license to operate?

1161.   Are there any regulations businesses must follow?

1162.   Are businesses required to keep records? For how many years?

1163.   How are records kept?

1164.   Do cartels exist?

1165.   How much smuggling occurs?

1166.   Is there a merchant class and how powerful is it?

1167.   What rights do members of that class enjoy?

1168.   Can people change professions?

1169.   How do people gain the skills needed to enter a profession? Apprenticeship? School?

1170.   How long is the typical work week here, in days and hours?

1171.   Do people take a siesta?

1172.   What professions do very well/poorly here?

1173.   What notable holidays or festivals exist and when/where do they occur?

1174.   Are there areas that specialize in a trade, being known for it?

1175.   Are there limits on how large a building can be?

1176.   If so, what is the limit?

1177.   Why does that limit exist?

1178.   Is there a typical floor plan?

SETTLEMENTS

The following prompts come from Chapter 6 of *Creating Places*.

1179.   What is the name of this settlement?

1180.   Are there any nicknames for it?

1181.   Will you set scenes here or only mention this place?

1182.   Will characters be from here?

1183.   Which races created this settlement?

1184.   Is the species that created it still here and dominant?

1185.   If not, what happened and how long ago?

1186.   How do they feel about this?

1187.   Which races have influenced the settlement's development?

1188.   What is the symbol or banner?

1189.   What are the city colors?

1190.   Do they have a slogan and what is it?

1191.   What is the settlement famous for? What's the first thing that comes to mind?

1192.   Are there any notable religious, magical, or technological sites here?

1193.   What legends exist about the settlement? Are they true?

1194.   What products does this settlement produce?

1195.   What products does this settlement need to get from somewhere else, and who is the supplier?

1196.   Is public transportation available?

1197.   What condition is it in?

1198.   Is it expensive or free?

1199.   What form is the public transportation (train, car, wagon, rickshaw, boat)?

1200.   How are messages sent?

1201.   Are messengers uniquely protected?

1202.   What historical events are important in this settlement?

1203.   What year was this settlement founded?

1204.   How old is this settlement?

1205.   What is the local attitude about magic?

1206.   About technology?

1207.   Gods?

1208.   The supernatural?

1209.   Are strangers welcomed or avoided?

1210.   What is the local form of government?

1211.   What type of mayor is here?

1212.   Is there a council and what is the mayor's relationship with it like?

1213.   What organizations or groups are influential here?

1214.   Is the settlement considered safe or dangerous?

Population

1215.   How large is the population?

1216.   What percentage of each species lives here?

1217.   What percentage are permanent residents vs. visitors?

1218.   Are any species outlawed or discriminated against and why?

1219.   Is anyone segregated and why?

1220.   Which race's culture dominates this settlement?

1221.   What is the overall disposition of the population?

1222.   What impression do the settlement's residents create for newcomers?

1223.   Do the residents seem to like or avoid each other?

1224.   What is the settlement's reputation?

1225.   Are there quarters, which ones (elven quarter, etc.), and where?

1226.   If so, what distinguishes each?

1227.   What important characters are in town, such as wizards, priests, and scientists?

1228.   Are any villains living here, secretly or not?

1229.   Are any heroes living here, secretly or not?

1230.   What monsters are nearby or in the settlement?

1231.   What effect does a monster have on the settlement psychologically and behaviorally?

LOCATION AND CHARACTERISTICS

1232.   What size is it (outpost, castle, village, town, city)?

1233.   In which direction is the farmland?

1234.   Is irrigation employed here?

1235.   Is there an Old Town, and if so, where is it?

1236.   Is Old Town well preserved or a warren of thieves?

1237.   What is the original water source?

1238.   What continent is it on?

1239.   What is the climate?

1240.   How does climate affect the way people dress and behave?

1241.   What land features are nearby?

1242.   Do any land features impact the ability of people to travel?

1243.   Is the settlement mostly flat?

1244.   Is the terrain hilly or rocky?

1245.   Where is the highest ground and what is built upon it?

1246.   Does the topography have anything noteworthy?

1247.   Where do the wealthy live?

1248.   Where do the poor live?

1249.   Is the pollution significant, absent, or moderate?

1250.   Does zoning (residential, commercial, industrial, agriculture, mixed) exist?

1251.   If not, are people aware of the problems thus caused and long for a better setup?

1252.   Is this settlement part of a sovereign power? Which one?

1253.   How important is this settlement within its power?

1254.   Is this settlement a capital?

1255.   Is this settlement in space?

1256.   If so, what is it orbiting?

1257.   How often is the orbit?

1258.   Is it on another body like a moon?

1259.   Is this an underwater settlement?

1260.   Is this a floating settlement?

1261.   If so, how is it protected from destruction?

1262.   How integrated with sea creatures is it?

1263.   Are there any sentient races/species that make use of them?

1264.   Is this settlement in the ocean, rivers, or lakes?

NEIGHBORS

1265.   What other settlements are nearby?

1266.   Are they friendly, neutral, or hostile? Why?

1267.   How big is each?

1268.   In which direction does each lie?

1269.   How hard is it to reach them or vice versa?

1270.   Are there any special or common escorts of travelers available?

1271.   Is there a cost for this or do taxes pay for it?

1272.   Is it safe to leave the settlement?

1273.   If so, for how far before trouble is likely to be encountered?

1274.   What kind of trouble is expected?

1275.   From whom?

1276.   What alliances does the settlement have with other settlements?

1277.   How many smaller settlements are near this one and partly dependent on it?

1278.   Is this the smaller settlement dependent on a bigger one? In what way?

DEFENSES

1279.   How much of it is surrounded by walls?

1280.   What are the walls made of?

1281.   How tall/thick are the walls?

1282.   Are there guard/archer/gun towers?

1283.   What other defenses exist?

1284.   Has an area around it been cleared of vegetation or anything else that aids an attacking force?

1285.   Is there a castle or fortress? Where is it located?

1286.   What condition is it in?

1287.   Has it ever been destroyed and is it now a ruin?

1288.   Is there a secret way into the settlement/castle/fortress? What is it?

1289.   Is the weaponry of this settlement superior to likely foes?

1290.   What sort of armed forces are here (knights, star fighters)?

1291.   Is there a garrison?

1292.   Are there any flying defenses? What are they?

1293.   Are there any defenses against flying attackers?

1294.   Is there a navy and which kind of ships constitute it?

1295.   How formidable is the navy?

1296.   Are there any restrictions on carrying or using weapons?

1297.   Are there training centers for warriors here?

1298.   If so, what kind of training?

1299.   Can anyone take the training, or only those in the military?

1300.   If the non-military can take it, do they need to pay in advance or with a service performed?

1301.   Are non-military treated differently and to what extent?

1302. Does the settlement conscript people into its defenses?

1303. Is everyone expected to play a role when there's a siege?

1304. Even women and children?

1305. If so, what roles do they receive?

1306. How old must one be to fight?

1307. Are women allowed to wield weapons?

1308. How much does magic play a role in the defenses?

1309. What war or battles have shaped life here, and how?

1310. Does this settlement tend to be the aggressor or the victim?

DAILY LIFE

1311. What religions are present here with buildings and worshippers?

1312. Are any religions shunned?

1313. Is there an official religion? How does it affect life?

1314. What religious temples and sites exist?

1315. What festivals or holidays are observed here and when?

1316. How easy is it to get lodging here?

1317. In what part of town do travelers stay?

1318. Is it safe there?

1319. What are some of the more prominent lodgings and what makes them unique?

1320. What guilds are here and what kinds of help do they provide?

1321. How well stocked are equipment shops?

1322. What sort of gear can/can't adventurers gain?

1323.   Are there any unique weapon, armor, or items that this settlement produces or has available?

1324.   How common is crime in the settlement?

LAND TRAVEL

The following prompts come from Chapter 7 of *Creating Places*.

1325.   What is the most common mode of land travel (foot, horse, car)?

1326.   What is the fastest mode of land travel available?

1327.   What is the least desired mode of land travel?

1328.   Are you using miles, kilometers, or your own measurement system? What's the term?

1329.   Are wagons or pack animals the primary method of transporting goods overland?

1330.   Do caravans happen?

1331.   If so, what vehicles (wagons, carts, etc.) are in it?

1332.   How big do the caravans get?

1333.   What kind of personnel are in it for protection, for example?

1334.   Are caravans considered safe?

1335.   Do trains exist?

1336.   How safe are they?

1337.   Can they be used for both freight and passengers?

1338.   What rideable animals exist?

1339.   What pack animals exist?

1340.   Do ridable animals that can specialize in fast or long-distance travel exist?

1341.   Are dirt roads common and where?

1342.   Are cobblestones common and where?

1343.   Are smoothly paved roads common and where?

1344.   Are bandits a frequent problem?

1345.   Are aerial attacks a frequent problem?

1346.   Are roadside inns/taverns available or unavailable in between places your characters will travel?

1347.   Does GPS or an equivalent exist?

WATER TRAVEL

The following prompts come from Chapter 8 of *Creating Places*.

1348.   How do you plan to use ships? Will scenes take place on them?

1349.   Are wooden ships a significant mode of water travel?

1350.   Do people still use oars to propel ships?

1351.   Do people still use wind powered ships?

1352.   Do engine powered ships exist?

1353.   Do submarines exist?

1354.   What percentage of ships are oar, wind, or engine powered?

1355.   Do wooden ships have cannons?

1356.   If not, what sort of long-range weapons do they have, if any?

1357.   What ship rates exist for wooden ships?

1358.   What sea creatures/monsters pose a threat to small vessels?

1359.   What sea creatures/monsters pose a threat to large vessels?

1360.   What sea creatures assist travelers?

1361.   Is there an industry for pursuing unique sea creatures?

1362.   If so, are those creatures hunted for sport, trophies, or to use?

1363.   What sovereign power(s) dominates the seas in different regions?

1364.   Where are the famous shipwrecks and why are they famous?

1365.   What myths, legends, and stories exist about the sea?

1366.   What's the name of the most renown pirate ship?

1367.   Who is the most renown pirate? Why, and where does he/she operate?

1368.   Are there islands known to harbor pirates?

1369.   Where are the most famous treasures rumored to be buried and what is there? How true are the stories?

1370.   What are the sites of the most famous ship battles, and who won?

1371.   Where are the dangerous and known reefs?

1372.   Is there a sea that no one has returned from sailing?

1373.   Is there an ocean that no one has reached the far side of yet, that people know of?

1374.   Do privateers exist?

1375.   Who is a well-known privateer?

1376.   Are letters of marque called that or something else?

1377.   Are there any famous incidents of a letter of marque not being honored?

1378.   If there are non-humans in the world, are any allowed or forbidden on ships?

1379.   Can they serve as crew?

1380.   If not, why not?

1381.   If so, are they assigned roles based on their race? What role(s) and why?

1382.   Are they respected and valued for the role they play, or feared?

1383.   Do they have any special needs on board?

1384.   Are there superstitions about any races?

1385.   If classes like wizards exist, what role do they play in ship life and combat?

1386.   Where are some famous shipwrecks?

1387.   What is famous about each?

1388.   Is there anything haunting them?

1389.   Is there any treasure there? What and how much?

AIR TRAVEL

The following prompts come from Chapter 9 of *Creating Places*.

1390.   Are there flying animals big enough for people to ride?

1391.   What is their weight capacity?

1392.   Are saddles required?

1393.   How do the reins work?

1394.   Can they be trained to follow verbal commands?

1395.   Are there special places where they are kept when not ridden?

1396.   How rare or common are they?

1397.   How much more expensive are they than other travel forms?

1398.   Is the average person able to use one?

1399.   Must people be trained?

1400.   Are the animals well behaved or nearly wild?

1401.   How cooperative is the animal?

1402.   Can the animal be trained for war?

1403.   Can they be trained to fly in formations?

1404.   How many can be reliably flown together?

1405.   If the rider is untrained, will the animal turn on them?

1406.   Is the animal inherently dangerous or only when provoked?

1407.   What sort of natural weapons does the animal have?

1408.   Do planes exist? What kind?

1409.   Do airships exist?

1410.   Do air balloons exist?

Space Travel

The following prompts come from Chapter 9 of *Creating Places*.

1411.   How common is space travel?

1412.   Is it affordable to the average person or only the wealthy?

1413.   Are only the military able to travel?

1414.   Does artificial gravity exist?

1415.   Can people only travel between a pair of planets when the planets are on the same side of their sun?

1416.   Does jump drive technology exist? Is it called something else?

1417.   Does hyper drive technology exist? Is it called something else?

1418.   Does warp drive technology exist? Is it called something else?

1419.   Is time dilation a factor?

1420.   What are the classes of ships?

1421.   Are there places that require ships to have insurance before they can be docked there?

1422.   What authority issues and recognizes insurance coverages?

A SHIP

These prompts are for when we're inventing a spaceship.

1423.   What is the ship's name?
1424.   What class of ship is it?
1425.   Is it possible to get this ship new or is it an older model?
1426.   What was the original purpose of this vessel?
1427.   Is it still serving that purpose?
1428.   If not, to what purpose has it been converted?
1429.   Is this ship used for deep space?
1430.   Expeditions?
1431.   Research?
1432.   Leisure?
1433.   Did this require any physical modifications? What were they?
1434.   From where do people and crew board the ship?
1435.   How many entrances and exits exist and where are they?
1436.   How can people get off the ship if these are blocked?
1437.   Is the ship intended only for space?
1438.   Where is the bridge located (front, deck #)?
1439.   Where are the crew quarters?
1440.   Is the ship large enough for a mess hall?
1441.   Entertainment?
1442.   A brig?
1443.   A separate medical bay?
1444.   What amenities does the ship have?

1445. What amenities do crew quarters have?

1446. Are there shops onboard?

1447. How extensive are the store supply lists?

1448. How much cargo can the ship hold?

1449. Does the ship specialize in carrying anything in particular?

1450. Are there items that can only be onboard if they're in the cargo?

1451. Can the ship take hazardous materials?

1452. Is there anything forbidden to be aboard the ship?

1453. Is the ship considered old or modern by current standards?

1454. Does the ship rotate to create artificial gravity?

1455. How many crew does the ship typically have?

1456. What is the minimum number of crew needed to operate it?

1457. Do escape pods exist? How many?

1458. Is the ship big enough for shuttles to dock inside? How many?

1459. Who is the ship manufacturer?

1460. Which species built it?

1461. What planet or space station was it built on?

1462. Was it built in space?

1463. Is this ship only sold to certain species and which ones?

1464. Does this ship have a noteworthy history and for what?

1465. Do people feel loyal to this ship?

1466. If so, why? What makes it worthy of that?

DEFENSES

1467.   What kinds of weapons are on board?

1468.   In which directions can the ship fire?

1469.   Does the ship have shields?

1470.   Are these physical shields or some sort of energy?

1471.   How strong are these shields relative to typical vessels?

1472.   How long does it take to activate shields?

1473.   How much damage can the shields take before they fail?

1474.   Do the shields fail all at once or can part of them remain effective when other parts have failed?

1475.   Is it possible to route more power to the shields to strengthen them or increase their longevity?

1476.   Are there different levels (light, medium, heavy) of shields?

1477.   If so, what impact does using heavy shields have on the ship, and which causes the crew to choose lighter shields?

OPERATIONS

1478.   What kind of propulsion does it have?

1479.   Does it also have air-breathing engines?

1480.   What fuel source does each kind of engine use?

1481.   Are there any delays in between deciding to jump to hyperspace, for example, and it happening? Why and how long is that delay?

1482.   What kind of vessels can the ship outrun?

1483.   Is there a race or species that covets these ships?

1484.   Does the ship have biometric controls that only some species can operate?

1485.   Can those controls be fooled?

1486.   Does this ship have a home base? Where?

1487.   Does the ship have any unique requirements that limit where it can be serviced or docked?

1488.   How rare are such places?

1489.   How does the rarity impact its usage?

1490.   What is the ship's current condition?

1491.   Are accident reports kept on these ships?

1492.   Are these ships insured? By whom?

1493.   How much damage can this ship take before it's destroyed?

1494.   How much damage renders it not worth salvaging?

1495.   What is the bare minimum number of crew required to operate the ship?

1496.   What is the optimal number of crew to operate the ship?

1497.   What is the intended maximum occupancy?

1498.   How many additional passengers can the ship accommodate?

1499.   What impact does this overflow cause on the ship's performance?

1500.   Can it only accommodate that additional weight in space?

TIME AND HISTORY

The following prompts come from Chapter 10 of *Creating Places*.

HISTORY

1501.   How far back does written history go?

1502.   Where did civilization begin?

1503.   In what directions did it spread?

1504.   Are there "ages" to the history?

1505.   If so, what defines them and when did they occur?

1506.   When was magic discovered?

1507.   When was each type of magic discovered?

1508.   When was each important technology discovered?

1509.   When was the first launch into space?

1510.   When was the first alien contact?

1511.   Was there an important magical or technological disaster and when? What happened and what was the aftermath?

1512.   When was the last major war, what was it fought over, who won, and what happened to the loser(s)?

1513.   When was there a great cataclysm?

1514.   Was the cataclysm natural (volcano, meteor) or not?

1515.   If not, who caused it? What happened?

1516.   Has a major sovereign power recently collapsed or been conquered?

1517.   If so, why?

1518.   How long ago?

1519.   What is the fallout from the collapse?

1520.   What important missions have been undertaken, by whom, when, was it successful, and what was the result?

1521.   When were important items invented or discovered and by whom?

1522.   When was an important item lost or destroyed and by whom?

1523.   If gods exist (or even if they don't), what are some famous events associated with them? When did this occur?

1524.   What impact did these events have then and now?

1525.   What supernatural or technological events shaped the present and when were they? What happened?

TIME

1526.   Do you want/need a different time scale to be a factor in your work?

1527.   Do you want time measurements to be like Earth's?

1528.   How many days are in a year?

1529.   How many months are in a year?

1530.   How many days are in a month, or does it vary?

1531.   How many weeks in a month, or does it vary?

1532.   How many days are in a week?

1533.   How many hours in a day?

1534.   How many minutes in an hour?

1535.   Is time measured like military time or is there an AM and PM?

1536.   For your universal calendar, what event is Year 1?

1537.   From what sovereign power did the universal calendar originate?

1538.   Do people know that?

1539.   Do they care?

1540.   Is a designation like B.C., BCE, or A.D. in use?

1541.   If so, what do the letters mean?

1542.   Since then, how many years have passed?

1543.   What are the names of the months?

1544.   Will you create month names that use seasonal words, and which differ in each hemisphere since the season is different?

1545.   Do the years receive names, too?

1546.   What are the names of the days of a week?

1547.   Do weeks receive names and if so, what are they?

Places of Interest

The following prompts come from Chapter 11 of *Creating Places*, when we are trying to create an interesting place to mention or have characters visit.

1548.   Is this somewhere characters will visit, or will it only be mentioned?

1549.   Does it have a name?

1550.   Is the site unique?

1551.   Or is such a site only rare?

1552.   Is there a structure there and what is it?

1553.   Is the structure occupied (if possible)?

1554.   Is the place abandoned?

1555.   Ruined? How much destruction has taken place?

1556.   How overgrown are the ruins?

1557.   What is still intact?

1558.   If it has a function, is it still functioning?

1559.   Has the function been changed to something other than intended?

1560.   Is the place feared or desired?

1561.   Is something or someone living there or nearby now?

1562.   Is it the creator, descendants, or an unintended guest?

1563.   Is the site revered?

1564.   Are only some people or groups allowed to visit?

1565.   Are there restrictions on when it can be visited?

1566.   Does anything happen to people who go there?

1567.   Is it dangerous and avoided?

1568.   Is it only special at a specific time of day, month, year, etc.?

1569.   Was it once special, and no longer is? What happened and when?

1570.   What makes the place interesting?

1571.   Is the place natural or not?

1572.   Did an accident lead to its existence or current state? What happened, and when?

1573.   If someone or something created it, who, why and when?

1574.   Where is it?

1575.   Can it move or be moved? Under what circumstances?

1576.   What does it look like?

1577.   What impression does it create from a distance and up close?

1578.   What is it made of?

1579.   Do people nearby know it exists?

1580.   Do they know what it really is?

1581.   How widely known is this place?

1582.   Does this place need an explanation?

1583.   Do you intend to reveal the explanation?

1584.   If the place is dangerous, has it always been so?

1585.   Has there been an attempt to change this? Did it work? Who did it?

1586.   If it failed, what happens to those who tried?

1587.   What species built it?

1588.   What species uses it now, and for what?

1589.   What secrets are hidden within?

1590.   Are there monsters here?

1591.   What was the purpose of the place?

1592.   How extensive is the layout?

1593.   If there are catacombs, what are the dimensions of most passages? What can and cannot fit in them?

1594.   Do the catacombs lead to anything, and what?

1595.   How deep do they go?

1596.   How long ago was this built?

1597.   Do they connect to anywhere else?

1598.   What famous monuments exist here?

1599.   Why are they famous?

1600.   Where are they?

1601.   Who built each?

1602.   What/who do they depict?

1603.   From what materials are they made?

1604.   What phenomena exist here?

1605.   What do they do?

1606.   How dangerous are they?

1607.   How common is each?

1608.   Are they guarded?

1609.   Where are they found?

1610.   Does the place give off a sense of foreboding?

1611.   Did something momentous occur here? What was it?

CHAPTER THREE

CULTURES & BEYOND PROMPTS

Everything not covered in the first two volumes lies within volume three, *Cultures and Beyond (The Art of World Building, #3)*, from where these prompts originate.

CULTURES

The following prompts come from Chapter 1 of *Cultures and Beyond*.

1612.   What name can you refer to this culture by in your notes?

1613.   Do you intend to use culture for culture clashes?

1614.   Do you intend to use this culture to depict places as differing from each other?

1615.   Do you intend to use this culture to define characters as different from each other?

1616.   What is the scope (sovereign power, regional, settlement, knights, royalty, etc.) of the culture you are creating?

1617.   What are the morals of this culture?

1618.   What are the values of this culture?

1619.   What are the beliefs of this culture?

1620.   What is the vision (refined, barbaric) of this culture?

1621.   What rituals have resulted? How often are they done and what do they signify?

1622.   What habits have resulted? Who exhibits them?

1623.   How has the government type impacted the culture?

1624.   What conflicts are typical for people of this culture with others?

1625.   If creating a culture for a race or species, what can you vary from population to population to avoid a monoculture?

1626.   What is the same across all cultures for that race/species?

1627.   What are the visible elements (style) of the culture?

1628.   What are the audible elements (tone) of the culture?

1629.   What are the behavioral elements (actions) of the culture?

SOCIAL LIFE

1630.   Are any subjects forbidden?

1631.   What subjects are avoided in conversation and why?

1632.   What is considered a faux pas?

1633.   Do people get married?

1634.   If so, is it religious or civil?

1635.   Do arranged marriages happen and is it the norm?

1636.   What are the consequences of avoiding an arranged marriage?

1637.   Can people elope?

1638.   Does common law marriage exist?

1639.   Are people allowed to divorce?

1640.   Are there people who may not marry?

1641.   What rights does marriage convey upon the individuals or their families?

1642.   Is having a child out of wedlock considered normal or bad?

1643.   How are bastards treated by society?

1644.   Do people have a duty to anyone? Why, and what is it?

1645.   What titles do people use to refer to the upper classes or aristocracy?

1646.   What occupations are respected or disrespected and why?

1647.   What are the daily routines of this culture?

1648.   What do they do for fun?

1649.   What is considered the normal family unit?

1650.   How do people view those who do not have one or come from one?

1651.   Do they use public transportation if it is available?

1652.   What side of the road do people pass on and why?

1653.   Is slower traffic supposed to behave in any specific way?

1654.   What do people think of those going too fast?

1655.   What are the expectations of those using public transportation?

1656.   What does this culture consider the most valuable trait, profession, or item?

1657.   Do people freely borrow items?

1658. How seriously are oaths taken?

1659. What are the consequences of a broken oath?

1660. What do people consider to be an ideal life?

1661. What gestures are common?

1662. What is the tone of conversation?

1663. What are common swear words or oaths?

1664. What slang do they use and for what?

1665. What jargon do they use and what does it mean?

1666. How often do people bathe?

1667. Do people bathe alone or in communal locations?

1668. Do they bathe in a river or private location?

1669. Is bath water reused by others?

1670. Does someone get to bathe first? Last?

1671. Do people sleep in their own bed or share one?

1672. Do married people share a bed?

1673. What do people wear while asleep?

1674. What beds do they have?

1675. How often do they change sheets?

1676. For the work week, how many hours a day per week is it?

1677. Is there a siesta?

1678. Are people paid for days off like vacation pay?

1679. Are holidays observed and which ones?

DINING

1680. Is dining formal or casual?

1681. Is there an established order for people to sit down at a meal? What is it?

1682. Is there an established position for people to be seated and what is it?

1683. Is there expected attire at various meals?

1684. How many meals are there in a day?

1685.   Which meal is considered the big family meal?

1686.   What meal is considered the private, more intimate one?

1687.   Which meal is the most casual?

1688.   Does an activity like afternoon tea occur?

1689.   Is anything forbidden at a meal?

1690.   Do people need permission to invite someone to certain meals?

1691.   Is it possible to overstay your welcome and how long before that becomes a reality?

1692.   How should a guest respond to offers of food, drink, or making themselves comfortable?

1693.   Are such offers made or are guests expected to make themselves at home without it?

1694.   What is rude behavior of a guest or a host?

1695.   Which foods and drinks are high quality to serve?

1696.   Which foods and drinks are inferior quality?

1697.   Do people eat with their mouth full?

1698.   Are there multiple forks, spoons, chopsticks, etc.? What do people use?

1699.   Do people double dip?

1700.   Do people wipe their mouth on a sleeve, tablecloth, or napkins?

1701.   What foods are only for nobility?

1702.   What foods are peasant fare?

1703.   What foods are a staple and commonly consumed? Why is that?

1704.   What is rare and a special treat? Why is that?

1705.   Is food typically bland or spicy?

1706.   Do people fast in this culture?

1707.   If so, is it for religious, health, or social reasons?

1708.   How long is the fasting in hours? In days?

1709.   What are people allowed to consume during the fasting?

1710.   Is there a celebration before or after the fasting?

1711.   What name is given to this fasting?

1712.   How often is non-locally grown food consumed, given the ability to preserve and transport food?

1713.   How is food preserved? Salting? Via magic?

ARCHITECTURE

1714.   What is the architectural style?

1715.   What impression does it create?

1716.   Are guests encouraged in homes, such as with areas designed for them?

1717.   Do homes have furniture for species/races of different sizes or other physical traits that differ from the host? Which races?

1718.   How many levels are typical homes and other buildings?

1719.   What is the preferred layout?

1720.   What shapes are tables and rooms in?

1721.   What are the most common building materials and why?

1722.   Is furniture slim and sparse or bold and large?

1723.   Are carvings or other decorations on furniture common?

1724.   Are rooms cluttered or filled with space?

1725.   How much echo is there?

1726.   How tidy is the culture?

CLOTHING

1727.   What clothing and styles do they wear? What do they signify?

1728. Are there any accessories this culture is known for wearing?

1729. How many outfits does a person in each class have?

1730. Is it common to see someone in the same attire all the time, even if they changed into another set of identical clothes?

1731. Is this one way that social classes are distinguished from each other?

1732. Are any weapons or accessories expected?

1733. Is there any attire or item that is rare?

1734. How is hair worn by each gender, child, and profession of importance?

1735. Is hair styled a specific way on certain occasions?

1736. How do people change their bodies with piercings, tattoos, or implants?

1737. How is eye contact handled? Is deference shown? Is a gaze challenging?

1738. What is the body language of this culture?

GREETINGS AND FAREWELLS

1739. When greeting someone or saying farewell, what words are said?

1740. What gestures are made?

1741. What Earth expression can you use as an analogue before modifying it?

1742. Does physical contact occur and what form does it take?

1743. How can a greeting or farewell be done differently to make it offensive?

1744. What questions ("how are you?") or statements are expected?

1745.   Are those questions rhetorical?

1746.   If so, what do people do or say if they actually want to know the answer?

1747.   How are casual and formal greetings and farewells distinguished from each other?

FOLKLORE AND SUPERSTITIONS

1748.   What folklore stories exist?

1749.   What myths (i.e., bad things come in threes, Friday the 13th) come from this culture?

1750.   What superstitions result from this culture?

1751.   What led to the superstition?

1752.   How widespread is belief in the superstition?

1753.   What lessons do the stories teach?

1754.   Are there characters or objects that have resulted from the stories?

1755.   If this culture is from a race, what elements of it differ between different geographical locations of the population (so that the entire race does not have a single culture)?

SOCIAL CLASSES

1756.   What are the social classes?

1757.   What are the defining traits of each social class?

1758.   What is the hierarchy?

1759.   What permissions and restrictions exist for each?

1760.   What prejudices does each class have about the others?

1761.   What is taboo? Why?

1762.   Do some classes have fewer rights than others?

1763.   If so, what is the reason for that?

1764.   Are people able to change their social class and how?

1765.   If so, how do those of that new and previous class view such a person?

1766.   What or who is considered a standard of beauty?

1767.   Are people able to meet that standard? Naturally?

SPECIAL EVENTS

1768.   Are birthdays recognized and honored?

1769.   Is there a party? Who is invited? What happens at one?

1770.   Are there traditional foods and drinks served?

1771.   What are the expected ceremonial elements?

1772.   Are individual birthdays celebrated or is everyone lumped together?

1773.   At what age do birthday recognitions stop?

1774.   Are children sequestered for any length of time after birth? What is the origin of that?

1775.   How are other anniversaries treated?

1776.   What do festivals celebrate and when do they occur?

1777.   What events or games take place at one?

1778.   What refreshments are served?

1779.   What is considered a personal milestone or rite of passage?

1780.   How do they differ between genders or social classes?

1781.   At what age is it expected?

1782.   How do people view failure to reach it by then or at all?

1783.   What are the customs around birth and death?

1784.   Is there a period of celebration/mourning and what behaviors are expected of whom?

1785.   Are there beliefs about what happens to someone when they die, and this results in ceremonies or actions taken? What are they?

ORGANIZATIONS

The following prompts come from Chapter 2 of *Cultures and Beyond*.

1786.   Do you intend to feature this organization or its members in your work or only mention it/them?

1787.   What is the name of this organization?

1788.   What nicknames does it have?

1789.   How old is this group?

1790.   What events led to its formation?

1791.   Is this group still around or defunct?

1792.   If gone, when did that happen?

1793.   What caused the group to end?

1794.   Why wasn't the organization able to withstand the event?

1795.   What happened to the group's members?

1796.   Did they form another group?

1797.   Is that group more successful in its goals?

1798.   What happened to the organization's holdings?

1799.   What are the group's defining values?

1800.   What is their vision?

1801.   What is this organization's goal(s)? Do they want to control an object, land, or have power?

1802.   How do they intend to achieve their goals?

1803.   How have they been trying to achieve their goals?

1804.   Are they willing to resort to violence?

1805.   Are they willing to kill innocent people as collateral damage?

1806.   How long have they been trying to achieve their goal(s)?

1807.   What setbacks have they experienced and what changes did they make?

1808.   Did they start off with a different goal than the current one?

1809.   If so, what caused the change?

1810.   Will the group continue after its goal(s) is achieved?

1811.   In what ways have the group dynamics changed because of any prolonged failure to achieve goals?

MEMBERS

1812.   How many people are in this organization?

1813.   What races/species are in it? Are any preferred or forbidden?

1814.   What is the group's symbol and what does it mean?

1815.   Are members given anything (pin, tattoo) to signify membership?

1816.   Are there factions with differing viewpoints within it and what impact is this having?

1817.   Does someone covet the leadership role?

1818.   Is the leader new or long established?

1819.   Do you need or would you benefit from the leader's position being tenuous?

1820.   Who is the current leader? Define them like a character.

1821.   How is leadership determined?

1822.   What traits are required to become a leader? Is that official or just the way it goes?

1823.   How does someone cease to be the leader? Death? Vote?

1824.   Who is the second in command?

1825.   Who are the leaders of any factions?

1826.   Is there someone in this group who is so disillusioned that they will become a problem, such as through betrayal?

1827.   Will they succeed?

1828.   Is the group large enough to have multiple subgroups in different locations?

1829.   Does the organization take prisoners?

1830.   If so, how are they treated?

1831.   Do members need to perform a task to become accepted?

1832.   Are there rituals or missions that must be undertaken?

1833.   Are new members fully accepted or on a probation?

1834.   Are new members assigned to someone whose approval is needed before fuller acceptance, and if so, what must they show?

1835.   Are members in for good, or must they establish their devotion/membership at given intervals?

1836.   Is the organization large enough to need a power structure?

1837.   If so, what is that structure?

1838.   Are people allowed to leave voluntarily?

1839.   Or are they killed for trying?

1840.   What do they lose if they leave? Access, items, contacts?

1841.   How does leadership ensure that the departing member does not betray the organization's secrets?

1842.   Is there a spy in their midst and who it is, and who do they work for?

1843.   What happens to a caught spy?

1844.   Has a spy been caught before? What happened? Are they a cautionary tale?

POSSESSIONS

1845.   Does the organization have a headquarters?

1846.   Where is it?

1847.   What is it like?

1848.   Is it hidden or in plain sight?

1849.   Do people outside the organization realize HQ is HQ or is it thought to be something else?

1850.   Is there anything special inside?

1851.   Is it guarded and by what? How do you get past it?

1852.   Can people live here? How many?

1853.   Can all the members live here or just a select few?

1854.   What are the criteria for permanent residency?

1855.   If someone can only stay for a while, what are the rules regarding that?

1856.   Is it only if they are recuperating or preparing for a mission?

1857.   Are newcomers required to stay here so they can be closely watched?

1858.   Is there a prison or jail here?

1859.   If so, is anyone famous or noteworthy in it?

1860.   How many people inside the organization know that?

1861.   Does anyone outside the organization know that? What would happen if people found out?

1862.   Does this group have any typical meeting places away from HQ?

1863.   Does the organization own any shared resources? What are they?

1864.   How is the usage of shared resources allowed or refused?

1865.   Where are each shared resource?

1866.   What condition are shared resources? Operational or in need of restoration?

1867.   What resources does the group hope to gain and why?

1868.   Who controls those desired resources?

1869.   Have any attempts to gain them failed? Why, when, and how?

1870.   What was the cost of the group for that failure?

1871.   Where does the organization get money to supply itself?

1872.   Does this group steal items to use or to sell? What type?

RELATIONSHIPS

1873.   Are there establishments (bars, hotels) friendly to them and their cause?

1874.   Are they banned from anywhere?

1875.   Do subgroups within go rogue or are they still on board with the mission and its means?

1876.   In what sort of locations can this organization be found?

1877.   Do individuals ever work alone on missions?

1878.   Are individuals/subgroups stationed in places for missions like reconnaissance?

1879.   If so, where and for how long?

1880.   Are any individuals, races, sovereign powers, or other groups allies?

1881.   Are any individuals, races, sovereign powers, or other groups enemies?

1882.   How strong is their relationship with each of their allies?

1883.   Are any of those relationships so tenuous that they cannot be relied upon?

1884.   If so, are there any actions the organization can take that will sever the alliance for good?

1885.   What actions can strengthen the relationship?

1886.   Why hasn't the organization taken them?

1887.   What clashes have taken place with their enemies?

1888.   Who considers this organization evil but is not an enemy?

1889.   Who considers this organization good but is not an ally?

1890.   What major events have happened in the history of this organization? When did they occur, and how did this impact the current state?

1891.   Has this group been driven out of any locations? Which and when?

1892.   What is the group famous for?

1893.   What legends or stories go around about them, and are they true?

1894.   What do people misunderstand about the organization?

1895.   What facts do people get right?

1896.   Do people donate to this group? Openly or in secret?

1897.   How does this group get along with each race in the setting?

1898.   What does each race think of this group?

Armed Forces

The following prompts come from Chapter 3 of *Cultures and Beyond*.

1899.   What type of armed forces are you inventing (army, navy, air/space force, or special like marines)?

1900.   Are you changing/defining one of those or creating something new?

1901.   What is it called?

1902.   What are its nicknames?

1903.   Do the members have nicknames (like "jar head")?

1904.   What type(s) of government do they work for?

1905.   What sovereign power invented them?

1906.   Where are they found?

1907.   What are their colors?

1908.   What do they signify?

1909.   What is their symbol?

1910.   What does it signify?

1911.   What impression does it create?

1912.   How do people feel when they see it? Relieved? Intimidated?

1913.   Which Earth military service are you basing ranks on?

1914.   Are you renaming the ranks and to what?

1915.   Does the military have its on judicial system?

1916.   Have they invented anything? What was it? How is it used?

1917.   What discoveries have they made and what impact did this have and on whom?

REPUTATION

1918.   What is their reputation among each race?

1919.   What is their reputation among each gender?

1920.   What is their reputation among those they protect?

1921.   Are there are famous stories about them?

1922.   Are any of the stories false?

1923.   What sort of light do the stories paint them in?

1924.   Are they respected by those they protect? Taken for granted?

1925.   How do they feel about this relationship?

1926.   Are they honored on any holidays? When and why?

1927.   Do they get special discounts?

1928.   How do those with whom they battle feel about them?

IN WAR

1929.   What battles are they famous for and why?

1930.   Have they won any decisive victories?

1931.   Have they lost any important battles or wars?

1932.   What terrain do they excel at traveling over or fighting in?

1933.   What terrain hampers them?

1934.   Do they hope to die in battle? Why?

1935.   What is considered a good death?

1936.   Do they have any typical foes, against who them specialize in fighting or defending against? Who/What is that threat?

1937.   How do they train to deal with it?

1938.   Do they collect trophies and what are they?

1939.   Are they honored with a recognized number of kills? What is it?

1940.   Is there a rank or bonus achieved by reaching a number of kills and what is it?

1941.   What is their fighting style?

1942.   What kind of ranged weapons are they trained in?

1943.   What kind of hand-to-hand weapons are they trained in?

1944.   Is there a type of fighting they struggle with such as plate armor inhibiting martial arts?

1945.   Which kinds of opponents give them trouble in combat?

1946.   Which kinds of opponents are easy for them?

1947.   Can they fight just as well on foot as on a steed/machine?

1948.   Which species/animals are harder to fight and why?

1949.   Which species/animals are easier to fight and why?

1950.   What special attacks do they have?

1951.   What special defenses do they have?

1952.   When defeating an opponent, is there anything they traditionally say or do?

1953.   Do they honor or ridicule those they've killed?

1954.   How are they typically used in war?

1955.   Are they saved for special moments?

1956.   Are they in the vanguard?

1957.   What famous missions have members of this military undertaken and what was the result?

1958.   How does this affect the way they are viewed today?

1959.   Do people remember such events, and in what detail?

LOCATIONS

1960.   What special sites exist for them and what makes them important?

1961.   How often are such sites visited?

1962.   Have any such sites been destroyed or captured by enemies?

1963.   Has this group tried to recover or rebuild them and how did that go?

1964.   Is the loss of a special site a psychic or emotional wound?

1965.   Are there special training grounds? What makes them special?

1966.   Are any training grounds famous and for what?

BEHAVIOR

1967.   Is there anything unique about their history? What, when, and why?

1968.   What languages are they required to speak, read, and write? To what degree?

1969.   What customs are unique to them and they are known for?

1970.   Do people salute them and how?

1971.   Are there any special handshakes or greetings/farewells, and what are they?

1972.   Are there any expressions they use before, during, or after battle?

1973.   Who does the leadership officially answer to?

1974.   Is there someone leadership unofficially answers to? Who, and why?

1975.   What is their relationship with every species/race in the setting?

1976.   How do each of those races/species view them?

1977.   Are they rivals with another military group regardless of location?

1978.   Are they rivals with another military group working in the same sovereign power?

1979.   What is at the heart of the rivalry?

1980.   Is this a friendly or hostile rivalry?

1981.   What caused/causes the rivalry?

1982.   How does each feel about the rivalry?

MEMBERS

1983.   Do individual members get nicknames? Are those more consistently used?

1984.   Who are the important historical members of this military?

1985.   Who is a revered hero?

1986.   Who is reviled as someone who let them down or betrayed them?

1987.   Are these people still alive and what is their role today?

1988.   Are there expressions about them?

1989.   Are there statues or paintings of them?

1990.   Who is famous among them today, and for what? What do they exemplify?

1991.   What races/species are accepted members?

1992.   Which races and species are forbidden or frowned upon?

1993.   Does racism, prejudice, or other discrimination exist within the ranks?

1994.   Of those who cannot join, how does resentment factor in their relationships?

1995.   How old must someone be to join?

1996.   How old is too old?

1997.   Are people required to retire or enter "desk duty" by a given age?

1998.   What skills and knowledge must people achieve proficiencies in and to what degree, before they can attempt to join?

1999.   What must they show to enter basic training?

2000.   What basic training is done?

2001.   How long does it last?

2002.   Where does it take place?

2003.   Is there a limit on how many times someone can attempt to join or undergo basic training or tests?

2004.   What skills must be demonstrated by the end to fully join the military?

2005.   What tests are performed?

2006.   Do the tests use real/live weapons/ammo?

2007.   Are the tests deadly?

2008.   Is it possible to bypass some training and tests? How?

2009.   How hard is it to pass the tests?

2010.   Must they change their appearance, such as a haircut?

2011.   What denotes they've been accepted? A pin? Tattoo? Uniform?

2012.   What sort of armor is given or expected at each rank?

2013.   What sort of weapons are given or expected at each rank?

2014.   Are they allowed to use their own personal weapons and armor or only that which the military provides?

2015.   Are there any weapons or armor they may not use? Does that ever change?

2016.   Are there weapons and armor that they look down upon using? Why?

2017.   If they have steeds or ships, are they allowed to use personal ones on duty?

2018.   How does clothing change with higher ranks?

2019.   Is there an occasion when recent members are publicly announced?

2020.   How much fanfare is associated with this?

2021.   How much compensation do they achieve and how does this relate to other professions in the setting?

2022.   How often is compensation given? In advance or after service?

2023.   For those who leave the military, what perks do they enjoy?

2024.   Do they take part in tournaments and contests?

2025.   Are they forbidden from participating in them?

2026.   Does the military stage those events?

2027.   Are they allowed to issue or accept duels?

2028.   Are there conditions on them, such as not accepting/refusing a duel to the death?

2029.   Are they allowed to issue or accept challenges?

2030.   What is the military penalty for violating these protocols?

2031.   How do they travel?

RELIGIONS

The following prompts come from Chapter 4 of *Cultures and Beyond*.

2032.   What is this religion's name?

2033.   What historical event (such as a prophet) led to the creation of this religion?

2034.   Was there a prophet?

2035.   What was the prophet's occupation prior to their divine revelation?

2036.   What is the prophet's story of interaction with the god?

2037.   What time of the day and year did this occur on?

2038.   What holidays have arisen and when are they?

2039.   What does each holiday signify?

2040.   How did the prophet die? Or is he/she still alive?

2041.   How did the religion react to this?

2042.   What did the god(s) do when the prophet died?

2043.   Which god(s) does this religion worship?

2044.   Is that god real?

2045.   Does the god(s) answer prayers?

2046.   What makes the god not answer a prayer?

2047.   What can improve the odds of the god answering?

2048.   Is the god capricious in answering?

2049.   Does the god only answer prayers of true believers?

2050.   What is the primary symbol of this religion?

2051.   What other symbols exist?

2052.   Are there any colors important to the religion and what do they signify?

2053.   What is the religion famous for?

2054.   If there's an official language, what is it?

2055.   What is the original language that sacred texts are written in?

2056.   Are there written texts?

2057.   What is the name of the most important written text?

2058.   Is there a sacred language that only practitioners are taught?

2059.   Is this a dead religion?

Behaviors

2060.   Are there pilgrimages to holy sites?

2061.   If so, how often are worshipers expected to make the pilgrimage?

2062.   Must practitioners fast and for how long?

2063.   Are there dietary restrictions?

2064.   Are there restrictions on behavior?

2065.   Are there restrictions on attire?

2066.   On travel?

2067.   How is a staunch believer determined?

2068.   Does the religion do missionary work, actively trying to recruit people?

2069.   Are they overzealous in missionary work?

2070.   How often must practitioners worship?

2071.   Does the number of times signify anything?

2072.   How many visits to a church/shrine must they make in a time frame (week, month, year)?

2073.   Are there any materials needed to worship (candle, mat)?

2074.   What does the material(s) signify?

2075.   Must worshippers wear anything specific while praying or visiting a holy site, and what is it?

2076.   Must worshippers wear anything and what is it?

2077.   Must worshippers assume a position while praying (kneeling, clasping hands)?

2078.   What does the position signify?

2079.   Is worship only formal, such as a priest conducting services?

2080.   How long is each worship session?

2081.   What is the goal of praying (atonement, showing faith, etc.)?

2082.   What customs exist in the religion?

2083.   What expectations, if not met, result in what punishments?

2084.   How strict is the religion?

PLACES AND ITEMS

2085.   Where is each special site?

2086.   Is this location considered holy now?

2087.   Is this location easily accessible because of terrain?

2088.   Is this location controlled by a sovereign power that restricts access? Who?

2089.   Is this location sacred to more than this religion so that it is contested land desired by others, too?

2090.   What items/artifacts did the prophet have or receive?

2091.   What powers do the artifacts have or are believed to have?

2092.   Which artifacts are lost?

2093.   Where are the missing artifacts rumored to be?

2094.   Where is each of the remaining artifacts?

2095.   How well guarded are they?

2096.   What happens if any artifacts fall into the wrong hands and are used?

2097.   Have any artifacts been split into multiple pieces, each hidden separately? Where are the pieces? Is there a treasure map?

LOCATIONS AND RELATIONS

2098.   Are there sovereign power types (monarchies, democracies) where this religion flourishes more than others?

2099.   Where does this religion struggle to thrive?

2100.   Is the religion influential anywhere?

2101.   What languages are they expected to speak, read, and write, if any?

2102.   What species/races may join?

2103.   What species/races are discouraged or forbidden? Why?

2104.   What is this religion's attitude toward each species and race in the setting?

2105.   Do practitioners believe any group is especially in need of "saving?" Which ones and why?

2106.   Does this religion have a contentious relationship with another religion? Why?

2107.   Are there any religions which this one gets along with well?

ADVENTURING

2108.   Are clergy allowed to join the military?

2109.   What is this religion's relationship with the military?

2110.   Is this religion non-violent?

2111.   Are practitioners allowed to join the military?

2112.   Does the military have priests from this religion as part of it?

2113.   Are the priests acting as counselors?

2114.   Are the priests acting as healers?

2115.   Are the priests involved in the fighting?

2116.   What kind of armor are the priests allowed to wear?

2117.   What kind of armor are the priests forbidden from wearing and why?

2118.   What weapons are the priests allowed to use?

2119.   What weapons are the priests forbidden from using and why?

MEMBERS

2120.   Has the religion developed any sects? What are they and how do they differ?

2121.   Does this religion have a recognized leader? What is their title?

2122.   Are there individual leaders at different locations and what are their titles and responsibilities?

2123.   What sort of power do these individuals wield?

2124.   What happens if one of them exceeds their authority?

2125.   Are there any individuals alive or dead who are especially important to this religion?

2126.   Does this religion have saints?

2127.   What sort of afterlife does this religion imagine?

2128.   Are the wicked punished or forgiven?

2129.   Are the good rewarded?

2130.   Is there a place like hell?

2131.   Is there a place like heaven?

2132.   Do they believe in reincarnation?

2133.   How many times can someone reincarnate?

2134.   Is reincarnation real or just an idea?

2135.   How does the religion prepare people for death?

2136.   What causes people to lose faith in this religion?

2137.	What causes people to stop satisfying the religion's requirements?

2138.	Are the gods believed to reward the faithful?

2139.	If so, for what are they rewarded?

2140.	What form does the reward take?

2141.	Must people die to receive the reward?

2142.	Is the belief in the reward accurate?

2143.	Do the gods punish followers for misdeeds?

2144.	What leads to a punishment?

2145.	What form does punishment take?

2146.	What can someone do to atone for a misdeed?

2147.	What role does this religion play in society?

2148.	Are people encouraged to only worship one god in this religion or are they allowed to have others?

THE SUPERNATURAL

The following prompts come from Chapter 5 of *Cultures and Beyond*.

2149.	What is the name of this supernatural element?

2150.	Does it have a nickname?

2151.	Is a nickname based on appearance or effect?

2152.	Are you inventing magic, radiation, a divine power, a place, or something else?

2153.	Does anyone or anything have natural immunity or resistance to its effects?

2154.	Is this a supernatural creature?

2155.	If so, from where did it originate?

2156.	What about it is supernatural?

2157.	What is it based on?

2158.	Are there supernatural beings besides gods, such as demigods?

2159.　　If so, how do they relate to the gods or other beings?

2160.　　Are there magic doorways or paths to get between places? What are they called?

2161.　　How dangerous are they?

2162.　　Who invented them?

2163.　　What precautions do people take before using them?

2164.　　Are they guarded and by what?

2165.　　Do alternate realities exist?

2166.　　If so, how do characters move between them?

2167.　　Are familiars part of this setting?

2168.　　How prevalent is the supernatural?

SUPERNATURAL ENERGIES

These additional prompts are related to energies.

2169.　　Is this energy widely available?

2170.　　Must it be channeled?

2171.　　Does it need to be contained, or should it be?

2172.　　What happens if it isn't?

2173.　　What happens to those who come in contact with it?

2174.　　Are those who can harness it physically taxed?

2175.　　Is special training required to manipulate it?

2176.　　Is special equipment required to control it?

2177.　　To capture or harness it?

2178.　　Is the energy only found in one place?

2179.　　Are its locations guarded and by what/who?

2180.　　Who arranged for its protection?

2181.　　Is the guard still active or has it failed and what happened?

2182.   What does the energy look like?

2183.   Is it visible with the naked eye?

2184.   If not, what is required to see it?

2185.   Does it make a sound?

2186.   Does the energy give off a temperature?

2187.   Can people feel the energy and from how far away?

2188.   What does it feel like?

2189.   Are any senses heightened or muted by it?

2190.   If there is a duration to this phenomenon, how long does it last?

2191.   Is there any sign that it's about to happen or end?

2192.   Is there any predictable pattern or phase?

2193.   Is the intensity constant or in flux?

2194.   Did this originate from an accident? What happened?

2195.   Did someone create this on purpose? Who and why?

2196.   What incidents have happened with this energy?

2197.   Which incidents are unknown or famous?

2198.   Did this energy cause anything to happen, like the creation of a monster?

2199.   Can this energy be used as a weapon?

2200.   If so, who figured that out and invented one?

2201.   Is the first use of this as a weapon famous? When was it and what happened?

2202.   Is there only one such weapon or has it been replicated, and by who?

2203.   What defenses exist against this?

2204.   Can this energy be used to power items, including vessels?

SUPERNATURAL LANDS

These additional prompts are related to lands.

2205.   What is this place called?
2206.   How easy/difficult is it to reach this place?
2207.   Is something magical or technological needed to reach it?
2208.   Is it in normal space/time?
2209.   Where is it located?
2210.   How does one get there?
2211.   Is it protected or guarded?
2212.   Is special equipment needed to survive being there?
2213.   Is access to it guarded and by what/who?
2214.   What arranged for its protection?
2215.   Is the guard still active or has it failed and what happened?
2216.   Does sight work differently here?
2217.   Are sounds changed in any way?
2218.   Is there a particular scent?
2219.   How does the place feel?
2220.   Is the temperature different?
2221.   What is the atmosphere like?
2222.   Is the air breathable here?
2223.   Are any senses heightened or muted while here?
2224.   Is this land permanent or does it come and go?
2225.   Is access to it permanent?
2226.   Did someone like the gods create this land? Who did it and why?
2227.   Was it the result of an accident?
2228.   Is it a naturally occurring place?
2229.   What is the purpose of this place if it has one?

2230. Do definable regions or areas exist inside this land?

2231. Is the land big enough for settlements and do any exist?

2232. Does anyone or anything permanently live here?

2233. Is this resident a native, or did they come from somewhere else?

2234. What kind of person voluntarily lives here?

2235. Does anyone involuntarily live here?

2236. If so, is it because they cannot escape?

2237. Are they a prisoner and of who or what?

2238. Does anyone or anything rule this land?

2239. If so, from where does their power to do so originate?

2240. Has it always been the same person?

2241. Does this individual have others working for them?

2242. If so, what people or creatures do so?

2243. How are they ruled and commanded? What gives the leader the ability to make them obey?

2244. If there is a settlement or building here, does it always stay in the same place, or can it move?

2245. If it can move, what causes this to happen?

2246. Is the new destination random or chosen and by who or what?

2247. Is there any pattern to the movements?

2248. Are there animals found here and are they different?

2249. Are the plants different?

2250. Are there plants or animals that are only found here?

2251. If so, what parts of them can be used for either magic or technology?

2252. How valuable are these materials?

2253. How hard are these materials to acquire?

2254. Are these materials forbidden anywhere?

2255. Is there a black market for them?

2256. Do people come here specifically to harvest them?

2257. How old is this place?

2258. What noteworthy events have taken place here in the past?

2259. In what ways did those events affect the current state?

2260. Is it expected that this place will cease to exist at some point?

2261. If so, what is going to cause that?

SYSTEMS OF MAGIC

The following prompts come from Chapter 6 of *Cultures and Beyond*. The term "wizard" may be used in place of practitioner, even if you go with another name.

2262. What is the name of this magic or magic type?

2263. What nicknames does it have?

2264. What name (wizard, witch, etc.) are practitioners called? Is there more than one?

2265. What nicknames are they called?

2266. Is this a soft or hard magic system?

2267. Are you modifying a known type or inventing something new?

2268. Is there a symbol associated with it?

2269. Are there colors associated with it?

2270. What is this magic type famous for?

2271. What stories about it are not true?

2272. What impact does this magic have on society?

2273. Is magic used for art and what effect does it have?

2274.   Is that effect just on the art or on the observer?

2275.   How do non-magical artists feel about this?

2276.   Is it so easy that they can be mass produced? Are there natural or legal limits on this?

2277.   Does someone need a license to sell magic items?

2278.   Do wizards stay out of politics?

Training

2279.   Is training needed to perform this magic at all?

2280.   Is training needed to master it? Or is training optional?

2281.   What aspects can only trained wizards [usually] do?

2282.   What kind of training is available (apprenticeship, university)?

2283.   What must happen before someone is accepted into training?

2284.   Do people have to be formally accepted somewhere to be trained in it?

2285.   What must someone do to pass training?

2286.   How common is a fully trained practitioner?

2287.   Does this vary by a criterion and what is it?

2288.   How much does training cost and is it something other than money?

2289.   Are there any training sites that are famous/infamous and for what?

2290.   Are there sites where something important happened with magic? What happened? When? Who was involved?

2291.   Are any races forbidden from being taught a type of magic? Why?

2292.   What does such a race think of being forbidden? Are they okay with that?

2293.   Have any of them become practitioners anyway, and how did they do so?

2294.   What happens to those who are forbidden from doing it if they are caught?

2295.   Is training done all at once like college and then it's over?

2296.   Is there continuing education?

The Practitioners

2297.   What skills of the wizards are famous/infamous?

2298.   What reputation do the wizards have?

2299.   Are wizards shunned? Why?

2300.   Are they welcomed as heroes? What have they done to warrant this?

2301.   Are they envied or feared? Why?

2302.   Are there special events surrounding the wizards? Positive or negative ones?

2303.   Are the wizards reputed to have certain character traits? Are people wrong?

2304.   What can the wizards do?

2305.   What can't they do?

2306.   Does society accept people who can do this or shun them?

2307.   Must these people live in fear?

2308.   Are there any famous practitioners in the past? The present?

2309.   What is their story?

2310.   How common/uncommon is the ability to do this magic?

2311.   Is the ability more or less widespread today than in the past?

2312.   What caused the change?

2313.   Is that change speeding up?

2314.   Has the golden age already passed or is it now?

2315.   Who are the famous practitioners and what are they famous for?

2316.   Are they still alive?

2317.   Is anyone a cautionary tale and of what?

2318.   Is anyone a hero? To whom?

2319.   Is anyone badly misunderstood and what is the truth?

2320.   Are these practitioners welcome in some societies but feared in others? What is a common reaction?

2321.   Does society honor them and how?

2322.   Are there customary ways they are treated?

2323.   How does one greet them?

2324.   Do they have a title?

2325.   Do they have ranks?

2326.   What must they do to advance through the ranks?

2327.   Is there any official governing body that confers rank?

2328.   Where is that body located?

2329.   Who is in charge of it?

2330.   Does it answer to anyone, such as the head of government in a sovereign power?

2331.   What is each magic type's relationship with each races/species?

2332.   How does each race view practitioners of each magic type?

2333.   How prevalent are practitioners in each race?

2334.   How well does each military group get along with practitioners?

2335.   Are practitioners members of any military and in what capacity?

2336.   How many practitioners are in each military?

2337.   Who is a famous living practitioner?

2338.   Who is a dead but famous practitioner?

2339.   What are they famous for?

2340.   Where are they now and what are they doing?

2341.   How did they die?

2342.   Are there any symbols of acceptance, such as a tattoo?

2343.   Are practitioners allowed to wield weapons and what kind?

2344.   What restrictions exist on possessing or using weapons? Why?

2345.   What sort of armor are practitioners allowed to wear and why?

2346.   Are practitioners expected to wear any particular garb and what is it?

2347.   What typically happens to wizards who are no longer at the height of their power?

2348.   Are there safe havens for aging wizards?

2349.   Does the ability to do magic change with age?

2350.   Is it possible to be a professional wizard?

2351.   What sorts of jobs do they have?

2352.   Are they well-paying and respected?

2353.   Are some of them considered crooked and untrustworthy?

2354.   Are there any ranks for wizards to attain and what are they?

2355.   What causes someone to rise to each rank?

2356.   Does this rising happen by itself or must it be approved by someone? Who?

2357.   What new abilities or spells are gained in each rank?

2358.   Can people fall in rank? What is the consequence?

2359.   Are there magical means of transportation? What form do they take?

2360.   Do they all require a wizard to be present, or are some a device?

2361.   What are the drawbacks of this form of transportation?

TYPES

2362.   Does black or white magic exist?

2363.   Does alchemy exist?

2364.   If so, are there multiple stages to it?

2365.   What is each stage called? What is its symbol?

2366.   What is distinctive about the alchemy of this setting?

2367.   Does witchcraft exist?

2368.   What is distinctive about the witchcraft of this setting?

2369.   Does necromancy exist?

2370.   What is distinctive about the necromancy of this setting?

2371.   What prerequisites exist for becoming a necromancer?

2372.   What specific skills do necromancers possess?

2373.   What sacred talismans do witches or necromancers possess?

2374.   Are their specific materials, such as blood or bones, that witches or necromancers need?

2375.   Do shamans exist?

2376.   What goals do shamans have?

2377.   Can shamans heal the spirit, mind, body, or all?

2378.   Does elemental magic exist, where a practitioner may only perform spells of certain elements?

2379.   If so, can anyone do multiple elements and what are they called?

2380. How rare is such a person?

2381. Does clairvoyance exist?

2382. Can practitioners see the future (precognition)?

2383. Can practitioners see the past (retro cognition)?

2384. Can practitioners do remote viewing of the present?

2385. Can practitioners also hear (clairaudience)?

2386. Do empaths exist?

2387. Is mind control possible (without spells)?

2388. Can people gain foresight by touching objects (psychometry)?

2389. Does telekinesis exist?

2390. Does telepathy exist?

2391. How rare are each of these skills?

HOW IT ALL WORKS

2392. Are there "schools" of magic and what are they?

2393. What defines and distinguishes each school?

2394. Are the gods the source of magic?

2395. Are elements the source?

2396. Is the universe the source?

2397. Is the solar system (sun, planets, comets) the source?

2398. Are other dimensions of planes the source?

2399. Can the source be exhausted?

2400. Does every species have the same source of magic?

2401. Did someone, like a god, make magic possible for the species/races?

2402. Was there an event that made magic available?

2403. When a spellcaster is summoning power, does the energy come from people?

2404.   The environment?

2405.   Themselves?

2406.   The gods?

2407.   What impact does performing magic have on the environment?

2408.   On the caster?

2409.   How long term are those effects?

2410.   Are there "natural" laws that govern how magic works?

2411.   Does the "school" of magic enforce laws or rules that are part of the magic system?

2412.   Can those rules be bent?

2413.   Broken?

2414.   What happens with the magic when the laws are violated?

2415.   What does that magic system cause to happen to the wizard?

2416.   What does the wizarding world do to punish the wizard?

2417.   What can magic not do?

2418.   How do people get around the limits?

2419.   Can two or more wizards combine their powers in a spell?

2420.   Can people perform more than one type or school of magic?

2421.   If not, why not?

2422.   Is it rare or actually impossible?

2423.   Are there a few people who've done it?

2424.   Are their identities known?

2425.   What is their reputation?

2426.   What is the physical toll of performing magic?

2427.   What is the mental toll of performing magic?

2428.   What is the social toll of performing magic?

2429.   Does training reduce these tolls?

2430. Are the results of magic predictable within defined parameters?

2431. Can completely unexpected results happen?

2432. What happens when a spell fails?

2433. Is gathered energy safely released?

2434. Are spells needed or can people do it by force of will, like a god?

2435. Are spells "typical" in needing words, gestures, and materials, depending on the spell?

2436. Are there places where magic does not work?

2437. Can such a place be created on purpose?

2438. Are these places random?

2439. Are they detectable before entering one?

2440. What happens when something magical, or a wizard, enters one?

2441. Do people with the talent feel different on entering a place where magic doesn't work?

2442. Are there places where magic is augmented?

2443. What causes them?

2444. How common are they?

2445. Are they known? All of them?

2446. Are they guarded?

2447. Is there a monster living off the energy there?

2448. Is there a magic language and what is it called?

2449. How difficult is the language to master?

2450. What impression does the language give when spoken?

2451. Is there a governing body for any types of magic?

2452. If so, who is in charge of it?

2453. How long do rulers rule?

2454. What qualifies someone to rule?

2455. Are any races unable to perform a type of magic?

2456. Are any races very well suited to a type of magic?

2457. Must people be born with the talent?

2458. Can the talent be gained? How?

2459.   Can the talent be lost? How?

2460.   Can the talent be regained? How?

2461.   Can magic be used as a weapon or defense?

2462.   How much has magic replaced technology?

2463.   Do magic items exist?

2464.   How easy is it to create magic items?

2465.   Is it possible to become addicted to using magic?

2466.   How does one escape from this addiction? Is it even possible?

2467.   What happens to those going through withdrawal?

2468.   Do people use magic for fun?

SPELLS

The following prompts help with the invention of a spell.

2469.   What is the name of the spell?

2470.   What are its nicknames?

2471.   For what type of school of magic is it?

2472.   Can more than one school of magic do it? Which ones?

2473.   What does the spell do?

2474.   How does the spell achieve its effect?

2475.   Under what circumstances can it be cast?

2476.   Under what circumstances can it not be cast?

2477.   What is the spell's reputation?

2478.   How hard is the spell to cast?

2479.   What level or rank does the wizard need to be to succeed?

2480.   How long does it take to cast?

2481.   How long does the spell last?

2482.   What happens if the caster doesn't do it right?

2483.   At what range is the spell effective?

2484.   Does the spell's effectiveness change based on a criterion like distance? How?

2485.   If it affects an area, how big is that area?

2486.   Is that area centered on the caster or at a point elsewhere?

2487.   Can the caster choose where to center the spell?

2488.   How many targets can the spell impact?

2489.   How much damage/healing does the spell do?

2490.   What words, if any, must be said to cast it?

2491.   What purpose do the words serve?

2492.   What materials, if any, must be used, how, and in what quantities?

2493.   What purpose do the materials serve?

2494.   How hard is it to gain each of the materials?

2495.   Is it easy/hard to keep the materials available?

2496.   What gestures, if any, must be made and for how long?

2497.   What purpose do the gestures serve?

2498.   Can the spell be cast without some requirements and how successful/dangerous is it likely to be?

2499.   Is there a race or species that has difficulty or ease in casting it?

2500.   Is there a race or species that is more impacted by it? Why?

2501.   In what ways?

2502.   What do they think of practitioners for casting it at them instead of something else?

2503.   Are there any tactics that can mitigate the effectiveness of this spell?

2504.   What is the cost of casting this spell? Fatigue?

2505.   How does a caster feel after doing it?

2506.   Do practitioners look forward to or dread casting this?

2507.   Are casters or others afraid of this spell? Why?

2508.　Are there stories about this being cast? What happened?

2509.　Is the spell legendary or overlooked?

2510.　Can the spell be used in ways it was not intended for and what are they?

2511.　Can potions be made from this spell?

2512.　Can the spell be put into magic items?

2513.　Are there limits on that?

2514.　Is the spell associated with a being like a deity?

2515.　Is the spell a cantrip?

2516.　In what ways does the spell become more potent when the caster is stronger?

2517.　Is the spell associated with a time of day, month, or year so that it is stronger/weaker then?

2518.　Is the spell associated with a season?

2519.　Is the spell associated with an element?

2520.　Which classes (wizard, bard, priest, etc.) can cast it?

ITEMS

The following prompts come from Chapter 7 of *Cultures and Beyond*.

2521.　Does the type of item have a name?

2522.　Does the item itself have a name?

2523.　Is the item ordinary or distinctive in appearance?

2524.　What does it look like?

2525.　Is the item supernatural/magical?

2526.　Is this obvious, like with a wizard's staff?

2527.　If it's magical, what activates the magic? What deactivates it?

2528.　What spell(s) is in it?

2529.   Is the item technological?

2530.   If magical or technological, can the object be used a set number of times?

2531.   Can it be "recharged?"

2532.   What are the limits on its powers?

2533.   Is the item worn?

2534.   Is the item portable?

2535.   If so, is its function solely supernatural or does it serve a purpose, like a sword, that is augmented?

2536.   If so, in what way(s) is it augmented?

2537.   Are there items that prevent magic from working within their radius?

2538.   Is the item sentient?

2539.   If so, how much awareness does it have through touch, feel, sight, and sound?

2540.   Can the item speak?

2541.   If so, does it do so aloud or through telepathy? Both?

2542.   Do you intend for the item to be lost and then found?

2543.   If the item is not magical or technological, what is its significance?

2544.   Who created this item? What species were they?

2545.   Who was the item created for?

2546.   How old it is?

2547.   Where was it created?

2548.   Were any special materials used in its creation?

2549.   Are its properties obvious even to one who has never seen such an item before?

2550.   Is training or knowledge required to get the most out of it?

2551.   Are there any hidden features and what are they?

2552.   Is a talent or innate ability needed to manipulate it?

2553.   Who has the item now or is it unknown?

2554.   Who is believed to have the item now?

2555.   Has the item fallen into the wrong hands?

2556.   Can the item be destroyed?

2557.   Does anything unusual happen when the item is destroyed?

2558.   Can it be recreated?

2559.   How common is the item? Is there only one?

2560.   How valuable is the item? Is that the value monetary or something else?

2561.   Is it possible to buy one of these?

2562.   As its inventor, how can you use this item?

2563.   How can your characters use this item?

2564.   Who, if anyone, is searching for this item or covets it, and how close are they to succeeding?

2565.   Does have any effect on the possessor?

2566.   Is that effect only when worn/equipped?

2567.   Does it influence those within a radius and, if so, how far from it?

2568.   Can the item be activated/deactivated and how?

2569.   Can those with a sixth sense detect its presence or true nature?

2570.   Are there any restrictions based on race, class, gender, etc.?

2571.   How is it used?

2572.   If the item is technological, how reliable is it?

2573.   How durable is it?

2574.   What typically goes wrong with it?

2575.   How easily repaired is it?

2576.   Are the parts hard to find or expensive?

2577.   How hard is it to replace?

2578.   Is the interface great or awful?

2579.   Are there third-party after-market add-ons available and what are they?

2580.   If so, what do they compensate for or improve? Or do they restrict it?

2581. How is the battery life?

2582. Can the item connect digitally to others and what is the benefit or drawback of doing so?

2583. Which technologies can/can't it interface with?

2584. What company manufactured it?

2585. What is the reputation of that company and their products?

ARTIFICIAL INTELLIGENCE

The following prompts can be used to create an A.I.

2586. Does the AI have a gender?

2587. Can the AI change gender?

2588. Is the AI audio only?

2589. Does it appear on video screens only?

2590. Can the AI appear as a hologram?

2591. Can the AI change its appearance?

2592. If so, are there limits on that?

2593. Is the appearance full-bodied or just a head?

2594. How pleasant is the AI? Or is it abrasive?

2595. Is that intentional or is it not programmed to understand reactions to it?

2596. How lifelike is the AI? Do people mistake it for real?

2597. Does it look real but its mannerisms or lack of personal warmth reveal its true nature?

2598. Is it capable of completely fooling even intimate lovers into believing it is not a machine?

2599. If so, are such AI common, rare, or never seen before?

2600. Are people aware that such AI exist? How do they feel about it?

2601. What type of systems can the AI interface with?

2602. How secure is the AI from data breaches and hacks?

2603. What safety measures are in place if either happens?

LIFESPAN

2604. How old is this AI?

2605. What advantages does this model have over previous or new ones?

2606. What disadvantages does it have?

2607. Is it considered outdated or new?

2608. Can it still be upgraded or have technology changes made that impossible?

2609. Is the AI aware that it is becoming obsolete?

2610. Does it accept that it has a technological lifespan?

2611. Or does it want to live forever?

2612. If so, what is it prepared to do to achieve that?

2613. Has it let anyone (or another AI) know of its desire or intentions?

2614. Is anyone helping it achieve such a goal?

2615. Is that illegal?

2616. What is the penalty?

2617. Has anyone tried to do that before and succeeded?

2618. Or are they now a cautionary tale?

2619. Is this AI known for glitches?

2620. Or slow boot up times?

2621. How does it act when something is wrong with it?

2622. Are there fail safes in place to shut down its access to certain systems?

PORTABILITY

2623.   Where is the AI normally housed?

2624.   Can the AI inhabit a machine like a robot?

2625.   Can it be transferred to another device?

2626.   If so, how long does that take?

2627.   How much of a technological match must there be for the transfer to work?

2628.   Do these transfers partially work?

2629.   If so, what elements are not present afterward?

2630.   What limits are there when it is not in its ideal or original device?

2631.   Is there a limit on how far it can move from where it is normally housed?

2632.   If so, is the amount of information taken with it less?

2633.   Can the AI be transferred back to its original housing?

2634.   If not, why not?

2635.   If so, is it fully restored as before?

2636.   Or is it impaired?

2637.   What aspects of it might not function the same anymore?

2638.   How much risk of impairment is there?

CAPABILITIES

2639.   What is the primary role or purpose of the AI?

2640.   What are its secondary roles?

2641.   What can the AI control?

2642.   What can't it control?

2643.   Can the AI shut off life support?

2644.   Is this AI the only one of its kind?

2645.   Is it a prototype?

2646.   To how much information does the AI have access?

2647.   Does the AI respect the privacy of personal data it can access, not revealing it to others?

2648.   Under what circumstances will it reveal it?

2649.   Can it fire weapons?

2650.   Can the AI anticipate actions or intent? To what degree?

2651.   Does the AI have directives it follows? What are they?

2652.   Does the AI have a directive about preserving life?

2653.   If so, does that extend to all life? Sentient life? Only some species?

2654.   Which species or race invented the AI?

2655.   Has the AI been restricted by its inventors in any way?

2656.   Can the AI be changed by those with the right access?

2657.   If so, in what ways can it be changed?

2658.   Who has the ability and permission to change the AI?

2659.   Who, if anyone, is in command of the AI?

2660.   Does the AI obey or only appear to do so?

2661.   Can the AI be turned off? How?

2662.   If so, how long does it take to power up the AI once again?

2663.   Are there self-aware AI who want to eliminate biological life?

2664.   Or reduce it to slavery or second-class citizens?

2665.   If so, how many of them? Is there an entire society of them?

2666.   Have they, in fact, taken over anywhere?

2667.   Are they on the way to another part of your setting?

2668.   How do they go about conquest?

2669.   Do they resort to war?

2670.   If so, why? Are they impatient? Destructive? Have superior technology?

2671.   Do they spread disease and wait for life to die?

2672.   If so, why? Are they patient? Vulnerable? Inferior technology?

2673.   Do the infiltrate and manipulate in secret?

2674.   If so, why? Are they patient? Vulnerable? Inferior technology?

2675.   Do they enjoy that?

2676.   How can they be detected?

2677.   What countermeasures have they developed to evade detection?

2678.   Is there a new way they cannot counter yet?

2679.   If so, who invented it and where?

2680.   How widespread is that new countermeasure?

2681.   What do their vessels look like?

2682.   Has this model AI, or this exact one, ever started a confrontation?

2683.   If so, what caused it?

2684.   What happened?

2685.   What was the outcome?

2686.   Is there a known vulnerability to this model?

2687.   Is there a known defect?

2688.   Does only the manufacturer know and there's been a cover up?

NAMES

The following prompts come from Chapter 9 of *Cultures and Beyond* and can be used for each naming style needed.

2689.   Do people have only a given name and no surname?

2690.   Do people have more than one surname?

2691.   Are there multiple given names?

2692.   Who bestows the given name? Parents? The state?

2693.   Are there cultural restrictions on the given names or does the giver have total freedom to choose one?

2694.   Are there any forbidden names and why?

2695.   How are given names chosen? What criteria is used?

2696.   Are they just given a number instead of a name?

2697.   Do people ever change their given name?

2698.   If so, is that official/legal?

2699.   From what or whom is the surname derived?

2700.   Does the state control surnames?

2701.   Is any name changed when someone hits a milestone? Which name, which milestone, and why?

2702.   If so, is it an insult to use their previous name?

2703.   Which name comes first when spoken or written?

2704.   How many syllables are given names?

2705.   How many syllables are surnames?

2706.   Are names so long that they are shortened in casual usage?

2707.   Are apostrophes common? Why?

2708.   Are hyphens common? Why?

2709.   Are silent letters common?

2710.   Do names, especially surnames, come from places?

2711.   From occupations?

2712.   From nicknames?

2713.   From given names?

2714.   Is it common to add "son" or "daughter" to produce a name like Jackson?

2715.   Are there any common articles used in names?

2716.   Are given names ever used as surnames?

2717.   Is there a letter or combination of letters that, when added to a name, denote a relationship to someone (father, employer)?

2718.   Is there someone (alive or dead) revered enough that their name is very common? What is that name?

2719.   Are nicknames ever turned into actual names?

2720.   Do compound names exist and from what are they derived?

2721.   If so, how much meaning or information can people derive from those names?

2722.   Are places ever named after people?

2723.   Are places named after events?

2724.   What suffixes exist (burg, ville)?

2725.   What prefixes exist?

2726.   Are there letter combinations that distinguish this naming style?

OTHER SYSTEMS

The following prompts come from Chapter 10 of *Cultures and Beyond.*

HEALTH SYSTEMS

2727.   What is the average life expectancy of humans?

2728.   Do people live long enough that they know their grandparents? Great grandparents? Parents?

2729.   Do the poor have access to health care?

2730.   Is there public or universal health care?

2731.   Does health insurance exist?

2732.   Are people required to have health insurance?

2733.   Is health insurance affordable?

2734.   How expensive is medical care?

2735.   Is there life insurance?

2736.   Is there long-term and short-term disability insurance?

2737.   Do vaccines exist?

2738.   If so, are they trusted and used or shunned?

2739.   When was the last major pandemic? What percentage of the population died, and where?

2740.   What was the most famous pandemic? Why was it famous?

2741.   What are the names of the more well-known pandemics?

2742.   If someone gets seriously injured or sick, is death likely?

2743.   Does supernatural healing exist?

2744.   If so, does that power come from the gods? Do people just believe it or is it true?

2745.   What other sources of supernatural healing exist?

2746.   What plants or animals have significant healing properties?

2747.   Are they hard to gain?

2748.   Are they hoarded?

2749.   Do the rich control them?

2750.   Which ones are most well-known?

2751.   What side effects do they cause?

2752.   Which ones have such serious side effects as to be feared?

2753.   Do antidotes to poisons exist? Which ones?

2754.   How rare is each antidote?

2755.   How strong of a dose is needed?

2756.   Have the concepts of germs and pathogens been discovered?

2757.   Are they widely known to exist?

2758.   Have sufficient preventive measures been put in place to prevent the spread of anything infectious?

2759.   Are there areas ravaged by infectious elements?

2760.   What areas produce new strains?

2761.   What areas are rumored to produce new strains?

2762.   Is bloodletting practiced?

2763.   Do doctors believe in humors or something similar?

2764.   Do doctors have patients do cures that are actually harmful but they don't know it?

2765.   How good are doctors?

2766.   Are doctors widely trusted?

2767.   How accurate is biological and medical knowledge?

2768.   Is childbirth still deadly?

2769.   Is birth control effective and available?

2770.   Is it legal in some jurisdiction but not in others? Which ones?

2771.   Can characters return from the dead?

2772.   Can people be resuscitated?

2773.   Is CPR known? Widely?

2774.   Can characters be reincarnated?

2775.   If so, how much of their memory do they keep?

2776.   Are mental patients incarcerated and abused?

2777.   Does psychology exist?

2778.   If so, it is a mature field?

2779.   Are there mental institutions?

2780.   If so, are they dark and terrible places or clean and peaceful?

2781.   Are there medications, technology, or magic spells that can help or cure, permanently or not, the mentally ill?

2782.   Is mental illness well understood?

2783.   Is mental illness shameful?

2784.   Do people hide mental afflictions?

2785.   Is suicide common?

2786.   How are the suicidal treated?

Information Systems

2787.   How are public announcements made?

2788.   Is there so much information that many people tune it all out?

2789.   Do people care about what is happening in the setting or think it doesn't impact them?

2790.   Is there so little information that rumors run rampant?

2791.   Who or what is a trusted source of information to each cultural group?

2792.   How much propaganda is there where the characters will be?

2793.   How informed/ignorant is the average person?

2794.   Are people unsure who to trust?

2795.   Do people have easy access to cultural information to avoid tensions in their travels?

2796.   Or must they rely upon a more knowledgeable character, and who is that?

2797.   Is there a town crier?

2798.   If so, from where are announcements made?

2799.	What level of technology exists for long distance communication? Mail, telegram, phones, radios, the internet?

2800.	Are these systems protected by sovereign powers or other organizations?

2801.	How reliable is the system?

2802.	How likely is a hack?

2803.	Are there any specific communication devices?

2804.	How reliable are they?

2805.	How easy are they to fix?

2806.	Are they precious or taken for granted?

2807.	Can anyone purchase and use the devices?

2808.	Are physical messengers protected or fair game for assault?

2809.	What animals are used to transport messages?

2810.	How are they trained?

2811.	How common are they?

2812.	Do messengers have any special privileges while traveling, such as discounts?

2813.	Is being a messenger considered safe or dangerous?

2814.	Do ships or stagecoaches carry messages?

2815.	If so, how well guarded are they?

2816.	Can magic be commonly used to disseminate information?

2817.	Are there magic devices that assist with this?

2818.	If so, how common are they?

2819.	What are the items called?

2820.	Are there any well-known, influential libraries? Where are they?

Legal Systems

2821.   What is the name of this legal system?

2822.   Is this a civil, common, or religious system?

2823.   If the latter, what god(s) inform it?

2824.   In what kind of sovereign power does this system exist?

2825.   In what kind of sovereign power does this system seldom exist?

2826.   Who presides over the court?

2827.   Who can be a judge?

2828.   Are judges respected?

2829.   Who decides innocence or guilt?

2830.   Are there lawyers?

2831.   Are people expected to speak on their own behalf?

2832.   Are witnesses allowed?

2833.   Is any sort of video testimony or evidence allowed?

2834.   Is there any supernatural evidence or witness allowed?

2835.   Are duels allowed to determine the innocent?

2836.   What rules govern a duel?

2837.   Must duels be sanctioned by an official body or person to be lawful?

2838.   Is trial by combat allowed?

2839.   Are people allowed to choose a champion to fight on their behalf?

2840.   What are the rules governing trial by combat?

2841.   Where and when do duels and trials by combat take place?

2842.   Is trial by ordeal an option?

2843.   If so, what is the ordeal and how is innocent or guilt determined?

2844. Are there any weird ways in which innocence or guilt is established?

2845. Is evidence gathered and used? What helps determine the veracity of that evidence?

2846. Can magic or technology be used to determine guilt or veracity of evidence?

2847. Are people allowed to observe any of this as if it's entertainment?

2848. Is justice carried out immediately?

2849. Are appeals allowed?

2850. How long do appeals take?

2851. Is the legal process considered cumbersome?

2852. Are lawyers or other professionals cheap or expensive?

2853. Do "public defenders" exist and what is their reputation?

2854. Are the identities of jurors protected?

2855. Is the legal system corrupt? How much so?

2856. Do judges honor or violate precedence?

2857. Are judges required to have an ability like magic, or is that forbidden?

2858. Are there separate legal systems for different species?

2859. Or different jurisdictions like magic?

2860. If so, how are these courts different?

2861. Who catches criminals?

2862. Who investigates crimes? Do they need any special training in magic or technology?

2863. Who pays those who investigate?

2864. Are there multiple jurisdictions and what are they? How are conflicts handled?

2865. Are people considered innocent until proven guilty?

2866. How are apprehended people treated throughout their incarceration?

LAWS

These prompts can help us invent specific laws.

2867. What is a common nickname for this law?
2868. What is the law?
2869. Does the law apply equally or discriminate?
2870. Whom does it discriminate against?
2871. What is the source of this law?
2872. Are you creating a law based on a moral or incident?
2873. What incident led to the law? Why was it bad?
2874. What moral has led to the law?
2875. In what jurisdiction does this law exist (local, state, federal)?
2876. Is this law enforced?
2877. Is the law draconian?
2878. How likely are lawbreakers to be let off with a warning?
2879. Are perpetrators considered dangerous?
2880. Is the law unjust?
2881. Is it considered harsh, lenient, or about right?
2882. Does it come from a different time in society?
2883. How old is the law?
2884. Is the law outdated? Why and what should change?
2885. What justifications, excuses, or arguments can allow one to escape or lessen conviction or punishments?
2886. Is paying a fine or doing a quest an option to escape punishment?
2887. If so, does the court appointment someone to join the quest as a witness?
2888. Is the law the subject of protests?

PUNISHMENTS

2889.   If inventing a punishment, does it have a name?

2890.   What is done to the guilty? For how long?

2891.   Where is it done?

2892.   Are people jailed?

2893.   What are the conditions of jails and prisons?

2894.   How hard are they to escape?

2895.   Where are they usually located?

2896.   Have there been famous escapes? By whom and from where?

2897.   Are people executed?

2898.   If so, what forms of execution exist?

2899.   Are executions private or public events?

2900.   Are any forms of punishment considered barbaric?

2901.   Is that okay to the society?

2902.   Is death peaceful or violent?

2903.   Is exile an option?

2904.   What unique punishments exist using animals of the setting?

2905.   What punishments exist using magic or technology?

2906.   Are some criminals physically marked upon conviction and in what way?

2907.   Can the mark be removed? Fully?

2908.   Can marks be placed on people who are not criminals?

2909.   Are criminals allowed to reenter society upon serving of a sentence? Or they allowed to be but considered second class now?

2910.   Is being forced to work a menial job a punishment?

2911.   Is restitution to victims expected?

2912.   Can people be banished?
2913.   Can people bribe their way out of punishment?
2914.   Are there societal classes that have traditionally evaded punishment or been given light sentences?

Educational Systems

2915.   For where (sovereign power, settlement, etc.) are you defining this education system?
2916.   Does basic education (grade school) exist?
2917.   It is available to everyone?
2918.   Are some groups (race, gender, etc.) discriminated against?
2919.   What form does that discrimination take?
2920.   How much protest of that discrimination is there?
2921.   Using an equivalent of your country, to what grade level does basic education go?
2922.   Is it mandatory? To what grade level?
2923.   Are parents or others punished for failure to have kids educated to the required level?
2924.   Does college or trade school education exist?
2925.   Are apprenticeships acceptable forms of learning?
2926.   If so, does a student live with their master?
2927.   Is home-schooling an option?
2928.   Do boarding schools exist?
2929.   What sort of curriculum is taught?
2930.   To what level is math taught?
2931.   To what level is the dominant language taught?
2932.   Are other languages taught and which ones?
2933.   How much history is taught and how accurate is it? Is there propaganda in it?
2934.   Are athletics considered important and taught?

2935. Is art and music appreciation taught and to what degree?

2936. Are more advanced subjects like biology, chemistry, and higher math (algebra, geometry) taught and do most people learn them?

2937. What magic subjects are taught so that most people are familiar even if they are not practitioners?

2938. To what level are technological subjects taught?

2939. Which education, if any, is publicly funded?

2940. Is private education available for all types?

2941. Are there public schools that are free to attend?

2942. Do taxes pay for public schooling? Is there a specific tax or industry that is taxed?

2943. Can one work a job to pay for school?

2944. For how long must one do so?

2945. Are scholarships available and what causes one to earn it?

2946. Must students live near the school?

2947. Does jurisdiction determine which school one attends?

2948. Do those living at school return home for holidays?

2949. For how many years is each type of schooling?

2950. How many months of the year is schooling at each level?

2951. How many hours of the day is schooling at each level?

2952. How many days of the week?

2953. What is given at graduation?

2954. Are libraries and labs onsite at school?

2955. At what age must students enroll in each required education level?

2956. Are there coed classes, dorms, and bathrooms?

2957. Are genders treated equally?

2958. Are species/races segregated?

2959.   Are some species/races not allowed to be faculty?

2960.   Are some species/races preferred as faculty of particular subjects?

2961.   Are any schools famous and what caused their fame?

2962.   Which school is notoriously difficult to be admitted to?

2963.   Which is school is most esteemed and why?

2964.   Where is most scientific, legal, and magical research done?

2965.   How literate are populations with this education system?

Monetary Systems

American dollars have been used in the prompts, but substitute for a currency with which you are familiar.

2966.   Are gems used as currency?

2967.   Are poor or high quality stones used for them?

2968.   What do the gems look like?

2969.   Are they carved or stamped with a design?

2970.   Are metal coins available?

2971.   What do the coins look like?

2972.   Are they stamped with a design?

2973.   Is cheating with metal coins, by including impurities, common?

2974.   Are coins milled?

2975.   Is paper money available?

2976.   Is credit available?

2977.   For each, how widely used are they?

2978.   Which sovereign powers or settlements are known for cheating?

2979.   What does paper money look like, including colors?

2980.   Are both sides printed on?

2981.   What is on each side?

2982.   Physically, how big is each currency?

2983.   What is the currency usually carried in?

2984.   What is the equivalent of $1? $10? $20? $100? Etc.

2985.   How many of what equals $1?

2986.   How many of what equals $10?

2987.   How many of what equals $20?

2988.   How many of what equals $100? Etc.

2989.   What words are used to describe each increment (penny, dime, etc.)?

2990.   Is the currency a unit of weight or unit of value?

2991.   If a unit of value, what is backing it? A power, settlement, or another body?

2992.   Do banks exist and are they backed by anything?

2993.   Do people trust banks or credit institutions?

2994.   Can labor be used as currency?

2995.   What gem or metal is considered the most resistant to fluctuation and the most stable investment?

2996.   Is the system a trade and barter one?

GAMING AND SPORTS

The following prompts can help you invent a new game or change one.

2997.   What is the name of this game?

2998.   What Earth game(s) does it resemble?

2999.   How popular is this game?

3000.   Is this a tabletop game?

3001.   Is it played on a field?

3002.   If so, how is the playable area defined?

3003.   How large is the playable area?

3004.   Is it played outside on the ground?

3005.   Is it played in the air?

3006.   It is played in water?

3007.   Are there professional leagues for this?

3008.   How well paid are players?

3009.   Is this a team sport?

3010.   If so, how many players on a team and what are their roles?

3011.   If so, are any positions more elite?

3012.   Can players be substituted and under what conditions?

3013.   Can a player who leaves the game return?

3014.   What skills do players (at each position) need?

3015.   Is training required?

3016.   What age ranges play this?

3017.   What happens if a player or a ball, for example, goes out of bounds?

3018.   Is anyone (species, etc.) restricted from playing?

3019.   Is anyone favored or have an advantage?

3020.   What social classes play this?

3021.   Do only elites watch it?

3022.   How well educated are audiences?

3023.   What items are needed to play the game?

3024.   What equipment do players wear?

3025.   Do referees or umpires exist? How good are they?

3026.   If penalties exist, what infraction(s) cause one?

3027.   What is the punishment for each infraction?

3028.   Is cheating rampant?

3029.   Are players unnecessarily violent?

3030.   Are fans violent when their team/player loses?

3031.   Is the game or sport known for civility or violence?

3032.   How are points scored?

3033.   Is there more than one way?

3034.   How is a victor chosen?

3035.   Are ties possible?

3036.   Is there an overtime?

3037.   Is the game timed? What are the increments?

3038.   Are there any tournaments?

3039.   Is a tournament at the end of the season?

3040.   Are there "major" competitions throughout a season?

3041.   Are there seasons?

3042.   What is the prize? What is it called?

3043.   Are there any famous players and who are they? What are they famous for?

3044.   Are any of your main characters former players?

3045.   If so, do some of their skills originate with this?

About The Author

Randy Ellefson has written fantasy fiction for decades and is an avid world builder, having spent three decades creating Llurien. He has a Bachelor of Music in classical guitar but has always been more of a rocker, having released several albums and earned endorsements from music companies. He's an IT professional in the Washington D.C. suburbs. He loves spending time with his son and daughter when not writing, making music, or playing golf.

Connect with me online

http://www.RandyEllefson.com
http://twitter.com/RandyEllefson
http://facebook.com/RandyEllefsonAuthor

If you like this book, please help others enjoy it.

Lend it. Please share this book with others.

Recommend it. Please recommend it to friends, family, reader groups, and discussion boards

Review it. Please review the book at Goodreads and the vendor where you bought it.

JOIN THE RANDY ELLEFSON NEWSLETTER!

Subscribers receive a FREE book, discounts, exclusive bonus scenes, and the latest updates!

www.ficiton.randyellefson.com/newsletter

Randy Ellefson Books

Talon Stormbringer

Talon is a sword-wielding adventurer who has been a thief, pirate, knight, king, and more in his far-ranging life.

The Ever Fiend
The Screaming Moragul

www.fiction.randyellefson.com/talonstormbringer

The Dragon Gate Series

Four unqualified Earth friends are magically summoned to complete quests on other worlds, unless they break the cycle – or die trying.

Volume 1: *The Dragon Gate*
Volume 2: *The Light Bringer*
Volume 3: *The Silver-Tongued Rogue*
Volume 4: *The Dragon Slayer*
Volume 5: *The Majestic Magus*

www.fiction.randyellefson.com/dragon-gate-series/

Ascension Quest Series

In this LitRPG fantasy adventure, a rock guitarist finds himself trapped in a VRMMORPG with only seven days to escape before he dies in the real world.

Volume 1: *Death Singer*

fiction.randyellefson.com/ascension-quest-litrpg-series/

THE ART OF WORLD BUILDING

This is a multi-volume guide for authors, screenwriters, gamers, and hobbyists to build more immersive, believable worlds fans will love.

Volume 1: *Creating Life*
Volume 2: *Creating Places*
Volume 3: *Cultures and Beyond*
Volume 4: *Creating Life: The Podcast Transcripts*
Volume 5: *Creating Places: The Podcast Transcripts*
Volume 6: *Cultures and Beyond: The Podcast Transcripts*
185 Tips on World Building
3000 World Building Prompts
The Complete Art of World Building
The Art of the World Building Workbook: Fantasy Edition
The Art of the World Building Workbook: Sci-Fi Edition

Visit www.artofworldbuilding.com for details.

Randy Ellefson Music

Instrumental Guitar

Randy has released three albums of hard rock/metal instrumentals, one classical guitar album, and an all-acoustic album. Visit http://www.music.randyellefson.com for more information, streaming media, videos, and free mp3s.

2004: The Firebard
2007: Some Things Are Better Left Unsaid
2010: Serenade of Strings
2010: The Lost Art
2013: Now Weaponized!
2014: The Firebard (re-release)